Lennart Björk – Michael Knight – Eleanor Wikborg

The Writing Process
Composition Writing
for University Students

To Mary K –
without whom it would never
have happened.

Michael

Studentlitteratur   **Chartwell-Bratt**

© The authors and Studentlitteratur 1988
Printed in Sweden
Studentlitteratur, Lund
Chartwell-Bratt   ISBN 0-86238-188-6
Studentlitteratur   ISBN 91-44-28221-4

1 2 3 4 5 6 7 8 9 10 | 1992 92 90 89 88

Contents

Introduction

This is a composition guide for students of English at university level.

We have noticed among our students both a need and an interest not only to be given more help in writing compositions but also to be given the opportunity quite simply to write more. There have recently been complaints about the inability of students to write in general and to write expository (*utredande och argumenterande*) prose in particular. These complaints are justified, but they should not, of course, be directed at the students so much as at the educational system which has neglected writing so badly in past years.

The Role of English in Sweden

Another factor we have taken into consideration when preparing this guide is the vital role that English, both spoken and written, plays in Sweden today. Restricting ourselves here to the written language, we have noted that Sweden is highly dependent on English for communicating with the rest of the world. Practically all international affairs in which Sweden is involved are conducted in English. Reports to the United Nations and other international bodies are written in English; many large Swedish companies have English as their official language, even within Sweden, as well as in their international business affairs, and any Swedish company involved in import and export will be obliged to write much of its correspondence and information in English; in academic and scientific fields it is almost essential for papers to be published in English if they are to receive international recognition. Finally, as a centre for international conferences and as a tourist country, Sweden also has a great need to provide written information in English. Thus there is a widespread need in Sweden for a high level of proficiency in writing English.

In brief, the needs of our students, both in the course of their studies at the English Department and in their future professional lives, have motivated this guide.

Writing as a Process

As you will see throughout, our approach to composition is process-oriented. That is, we see composition not from the reader's point of view but from the writer's standpoint, since we are concerned here with helping students to improve their writing. Thus we emphasize the various stages all writers go through before arriving at their final version, and provide many opportunities for practising these various stages. We do so because it is being increasingly recognised in the teaching of composition that writing is not just a question of finding words for a set of ready-made ideas. It is instead a method for finding and working out what it is we want to say. In the process of rewriting our compositions (i.e. writing several drafts) we find out what our ideas are and where they need more attention. We add new ones, abandon some old ones and then gradually decide what order to arrange them in. Working one's way through a series of drafts is also a way of deciding what are the best words to use and what sentence and paragraph arrangement will be clearest.

You will notice that we advise students in the early stages of their work not to spend too much time worrying about language correctness. This is because we now know that obsession with correctness at these first stages makes it difficult for the writer to work out what (s)he wants to say. In other words, early drafts are a place for thinking on paper. Once the writer has decided what (s)he wants to say, his/her mind is free to concentrate on correctness, which is of course essential for the success of the final version of a composition.

We advocate this method of teaching writing because it has proved very successful elsewhere in the past decade. In particular our optimism derives from the spectacular success of the Bay Area Writing Project at the University of California, Berkeley. We are greatly indebted to its director, James Gray, and co-director, Mary K Healy, for their invaluable assistance in getting our writing programme started.

We are most grateful to the Educational Development Unit (PU-enheten) at Stockholm University for grants which have enabled us to develop and test our material.

We should also like to thank our colleagues and students who, in various ways, with contributions and comments, have helped us in the preparation of this guide: Catherine Dahlström, Nils-Lennart Johannesson, Anne-Charlotte Lindeberg, Ishrat Lindblad, Ingela Löfgren, Mats Pettersson, Pamela Rees-Björnberg and Rita Russell.

Not least we would like to thank Ann Wallin and Ingegerd Folcker for their swift and accurate typing.

Stockholm, August 1988

Lennart Björk – Michael Knight – Eleanor Wikborg

Suggestions for Using this Guide

This guide can be used either in class with a teacher or for private study. The Key to the Exercises at the end of the book makes it possible for students to work by themselves, but classwork with a teacher's guidance is obviously preferable.

As we said in the Introduction, the main theme of this book is that writing, seen from the writer's point of view, is a process. In other words, a composition takes time and needs to go through several stages before it becomes a finished product fit to be handed in.

The following chapters will take you step by step through these various stages; each chapter begins with an explanation of why we recommend certain strategies and techniques, and continues with a number of exercises and writing tasks. In this way we give you both advice and systematic practice at every stage throughout the course.

In general we suggest that you begin at the beginning and work through each chapter in turn, with the exception of Chapter V and the Appendices, which should be used for reference throughout. The section on spoken and written English and formal and informal writing, with the follow-up discussion, makes a useful introduction to the general question of what writing involves. Then, in Chapter I, we suggest that you begin with writing based on personal experience. This fairly informal kind of composition will show you how to use writing as a way of sorting out your ideas (see letter on page 10), and how to organise these ideas in short compositions.

Dear Ann:

I'm a 26-year-old woman and I feel like a fool asking you this question, but — should I marry the guy or not? Jerry is 30, but sometimes he acts like 14. We have gone together for nearly a year. He was married for three years but never talks about it. My parents haven't said anything for or against him, but I know deep down they don't like him much.

Jerry is a salesman and makes good money but has lost his wallet three times since I've known him and I've had to help him meet the payments on his car.

The thing that bothers me most, I think, is that I have the feeling he doesn't trust me. After every date he telephones. He says it's to ''say an extra goodnight'', but I'm sure he is checking to see if I had a late date with someone else.

One night I was in the shower and didn't hear the phone. He came over and sat on the porch all night. I found him asleep on the swing when I went to get the paper the next morning at 6:30 a.m. I had a hard time convincing him I had been in the house the whole time.

Now on the plus side: Jerry is very good-looking and appeals to me physically. Well — that does it. I have been sitting here with this pen in my hand for 15 minutes trying to think of something else good to say about him and nothing comes to mind.

Don't bother to answer this. You have helped me more than you will ever know.

Yours,

Eyes Opened

An example of the way writing can help you to "sort out your ideas".

Chapter II presents the general sequence of work that we suggest:

Generate ideas
Write first draft
Response group work
Write second draft
Teacher's response (optional)
Edit
Hand in final version

Response groups are where you try out your first drafts on some classmates. At first you will need to practise in class, but we recommend you to go on working in pairs or small groups outside the classroom as well.

Chapter III shows you how to achieve unity and coherence in the paragraph, and begins with public debate writing, that is, compositions on subjects of general social and cultural interest such as one reads about in newspapers and magazines. We have chosen to put public debate writing first because it makes use of a common basis of knowledge which all students will be familiar with, and is thus more easily dealt with in the class as a whole. If, however, the class is studying a particular book, this too will provide a common basis for discussion and writing, and in this case writing about books may well be given pride of place before public debate writing.

Whether you move from personal experience writing to public debate writing or to writing about literature, we suggest that you always use the sequence of work given above; and that you refer to Chapter V, Editing before completing your composition and handing it in.

The Appendices contain short sample compositions and a list of composition subjects for further writing.

Follow-up

May we suggest three kinds of follow-up work to writing:

1 Discuss in class mistakes that come up in your compositions ("The Rogues' Gallery"). These mistakes may include any aspect of the written language: grammar, vocabulary, spelling, punctuation and lay-out, but also problems of ambiguity, tautology and irrelevance.

2 If your composition needs a great deal of correction, we suggest you rewrite it completely, with the help of your teacher's comments. The vastly

improved version which will result will be encouraging for both you and your teacher. In fact, rewriting is probably the most effective way of improving your composition writing. Practically all great writers rewrite continuously, so why not you!

3 We would very strongly encourage you to read each other's compositions. This is up to you, of course, but collaboration is fun, and a great deal can be learnt from both the well-written and the not-so-well-written composition. The existence of an audience besides teacher also provides motivation for writing.

4 If possible, publish a magazine or wall-sheet on themes like "A Person Who Meant a Lot to Me", "Unemployment among Young People" or "The Character of Ralph in *Lord of the Flies*". Again, knowing that there is a wider audience for your writing will be highly motivating.

Spoken and Written English

It is important to realize that spoken and written English are different. In spite of what the Swedish Post Office has said, written language is not merely spoken language written down. The main reason is that speaking and writing take place in different circumstances. Normally when you speak, you are face to face with someone; when you write, you do not have your reader in front of you. In fact, unless you are writing a letter, you probably do not even know who your reader or readers will be – except at school, where you write for "teacher".

These differences affect the way you use language. In a face-to-face situation you can see immediately whether your audience is following you, and they can usually interrupt to ask a question or confirm a point. There is constant interaction between speaker and listener. This means that a speaker does not need to organize his language so strictly and coherently. The feedback he gets from his audience tells him immediately when he has not been understood. A writer, however, does not get this immediate feedback, so he must organize his language so that the reader can follow his thoughts without difficulty. A reader should not have to be a mind-reader. All the time as a writer you must put yourself in your reader's shoes. There must be no danger of his misunderstanding what you have written, or of not being able to follow your thoughts.

To achieve this aim, the written language has a number of devices that are vital for effective communication. In addition to such obvious features as spelling and punctuation, they include the clear use of back references - a pronoun, for example, must refer clearly to a particular noun already mentioned – and coherence, the logical linking and development of ideas within and between sentences. We shall be dealing with these devices in detail in Chapter III.

Another big difference between speaking and writing is that speech has to be instantaneous, while writing can and usually does take time to complete. Thus you should think of writing not only as a finished product but also as a process, a process of gradually working out what you want to say in writing.

One of our main themes in this guide will be that there are no "instant" compositions, but that all writing needs to go through several stages in the process of becoming a completed composition.

A further difference between speaking and writing is that speech is ephemeral, it disappears as soon as it is produced (unless you record it on tape), while writing is permanent. This means that you can work on a piece of writing for as long as you like, leaving it and coming back to it, going back in it as far as you like, changing it as often as you like. This is the great advantage of writing over speech. It allows time for thought and improvement. But it also means that a higher standard of coherence and correctness is expected in a piece of finished writing than in speech.

Finally, there are certain conventions of style that distinguish the language of expository writing from most spoken language. You can think of these as a kind of etiquette, if you like. And just as it is not good etiquette to go to a wedding dressed in jeans and wellingtons, it is not acceptable to use a colloquial style in formal writing - unless you want to create a very special effect! Besides, wellingtons are not very practical if you are going to dance, and the same can be said of colloquial style in an expository composition. Some of the more obvious conventions of style are listed in Chapter V, and to become a competent writer you will need to follow them. Only acknowledged experts can afford to break conventions.

The special nature of writing thus means that you will not necessarily be a good writer just because you speak English fluently. Even native English speakers have to spend years learning the special demands and conventions of writing. However, being a fluent speaker makes a good starting point, and we are lucky enough in Sweden to be able to presume that you are a relatively fluent speaker of English. This guide will, we hope, help you to become a more effective writer of English by utilising your existing fluency in the language.

Formal and Informal Writing

There is one last important point we should like to make about written English. What we have said above refers to formal written English, the kind of writing that we want to teach you to write – that is, writing intended for "public consumption". This does not include diaries, post-cards and love-letters, for example. Nor does it include the preliminary stages of formal writing: journals, notes and first drafts. These types of writing are informal, they are intended for your personal use, and do not therefore demand the same degree of coherence and correctness as formal writing. In this guide we approach formal writing through speech and informal writing; thus the first section gets you to discuss and write informally on a number of subjects. This is one of the most effective means of achieving our final goal, the kind of writing that you will need to produce in your professional life: writing that is clear, coherent and correct and which communicates effectively.

Points to discuss

1 Do you feel that you speak better English than you write it?
2 What difficulties have you noticed when you have written something in English? When you have finished your discussion, look at Appendix I, p 118 "The Agony of Composition Writing".
3 What differences do you first think of when you compare, say, a conversation and an article in a magazine?
4 Why is it that some pieces of writing are more difficult to understand than others?

I Generating Ideas

Writing as Communication

We all know how difficult it is to write. "I have nothing to say," we protest, or else: "I know what I want to say, but I just can't get it right!" Experienced writers struggle hard to "get it right". Even the happy periods when the words just flow are preceded by the long hard slog of generating ideas, making notes and thinking things out.

But even if you are one of those who will do anything to postpone putting pen to paper, you will discover, to your surprise, how well you write, how excited you feel when you have something you really want to communicate to someone else. This is true of both personal and professional writing. Although a letter to a friend analysing the reasons for a quarrel will be more personal than a report to the Student Union on the reasons why the cafeteria should be open on Saturdays, in both cases you will be personally involved in what you are writing.

Unfortunately, it is not always easy to feel so involved, so motivated when writing at school or university. The compositions you write there often seem to be more for practising language than for communicating ideas. This lack of enthusiasm has a very negative effect on writing skills, because it is only when you feel committed to what you write that you will want to and be able to express yourself accurately and effectively.

For these reasons it is important when you write a composition to begin by drawing on the rich store of ideas, information, feelings and curiosity which you have gained from your experience of living and studying. This chapter presents four techniques which will help you to discover what it is you want to say on a subject and put you on the right track for a successful piece of writing. They are Journal Writing, Brainstorming, Clustering and Interviewing.

Journal Writing

A journal is an informal record of your reactions to your studies: to the books you are reading, to the lectures you are attending and to the class discussions you are taking part in. We use the term journal rather than diary since it deals with your English studies rather than your private life. In fact, a journal is a personal record of your reactions to your English studies, both in class and while studying at home.

Here is an example of a short journal entry:

Journal Entry on a Language Class

We went through the homework – Future Tenses. Interesting to discuss alternatives for different styles of writing. Obviously there are many ways of talking about the future in English. Actually the rules seem more complicated than the examples. Still don't really understand the difference between "is to" and "is going to", especially in If sentences. But now I know – I think – that "shall" is only used in questions or in the Bible "Thou shalt not commit adultery". What about "will"? – "I shall" or "I will"? Ask next time.

You will find some more examples of journals on pages 19–20.

Reasons for Journal Writing

There are several reasons why we suggest you keep a journal. First, the regular experience of writing down your ideas will stimulate your overall intellectual growth. It is a well-known fact that writing itself generates new ideas and feelings. A few sessions with your journal will prove to you that this is so.

Second, writing down your ideas helps you to clarify and organize them. You will discover as you write what interests you or puzzles you or annoys you. Writing down ideas will trigger a desire to find out why a certain problem or character fascinated or baffled you, or how a certain group of facts are logically connected. You will discover important points that you will be able to bring up later in an organized way in class. Writing down ideas is, in fact, an excellent way of preparing for a class discussion.

Third, and most important to you as a language student, writing regularly will give you many opportunities to improve your English. One of the main problems you face when writing English is to find the right words and phrases to express your thoughts. The only answer to this problem is constant practice. Journal writing gives you the opportunity to express your ideas regularly without the stress of having to write a long formal composition. By de-dramatising the business of writing it will give you a chance to write "little and often", which is one of the best ways of improving your English.

Fourth, journal writing is an invaluable learning aid. The process of writing down what you have learnt not only helps you to remember it; it also enables you to link the new language and ideas with what you know already, and in this way make them your own. And writing is something you can do by yourself at any time. You do not need anything more than a pencil and a sheet of paper. A journal entry can be just a few notes jotted down at the end of a study session or maybe later, when you can see things in a different perspective; or it can be much longer, exploring for example various aspects of a novel you are studying.

So we would like to encourage you to keep a journal regularly, which means writing at least once a week. You can either write your entries on loose sheets which you put in a file or you can have a special Journal Book for your entries.

Examples of Journal Entries

On reading Doris Lessing's short story "Flight"

Why does the grandfather act and react the way he does? Why is he so angry over the fact that the girl is getting married? He behaves very childishly in his attempts to prevent the marriage. It is almost as if he was jealous. Still, he thinks of her, too. He wants her to be free, at least for some time before getting tied down with a husband and child. Perhaps his birds, and their lack of freedom, symbolize the grandfather's situation? After he lets his birds out for a short flight at the end, the granddaughter cries – why? Must think more about this.

Class Discussion of *Lord of the Flies*

Today's class on Golding's novel an exciting experience. Discussed what Lennart quoted as "the thin veneer of civilization".

Ralph an average boy for his age I guess – perhaps for any human being who has not met with much human evil.

Piggy – disgusting looks and habits, but fine human being. Lena said he was the typical schoolboy who sticks to all the rules – she could understand why he irritated the others. But I think he was right. Without rules, they would just turn into fighting animals. Besides, I don't think Piggy irritated anybody but Jack. Or did he? Must check that. Anyway, *why* did Jack attack Piggy so much?

Lennart went through animal imagery too quickly for some of us. I couldn't find a couple of examples in the middle of the book. I'm not sure what an image is. It's a picture of some kind that compares. Maybe like Piggy being like a pig (fat, pink, ugly – aren't pigs clever too?)??

Lecture on Education in England

English school-system seems strange at first. Terminology (?) confusing: "public" schools meaning *private*. Typically English (but D. suspects I'm prejudiced perhaps even anti-English, not true, of course).

I like the elite system in England – it can't be as bad as D. says. We need to take care of our *best* students as well. All is nonsense about justice. Of course it's not just that some students are better than others. That is no reason to keep the best ones back. I don't mean that money should decide who goes to university and who doesn't. Ability should decide.

How can England manage to give *all* students grants? Here we have to borrow money. We have a higher percentage of university students, though the number is being cut. Must try to read *The History Man* Malcolm Bradbury (not Ray). Perhaps we should have tutors. Could we afford them?

Journal writing has one more valuable function. It can become a channel for communication with your teacher. You may feel hesitant about asking questions, raising objections or making comments in class. A journal provides a more private means of communication. As well as giving you an opportunity to "talk" to your teacher it will give your teacher insight into your particular difficulties, thus making the teaching more effective to the benefit of all concerned.

For this reason you will be asked to hand in your journal at regular intervals throughout the term. But it is a confidential document. It will not be shown to, or discussed with other teachers. However, if you give your permission, points raised in your journal may be discussed in class.

Finally, remember that journal writing is *informal* writing. Your ideas are the main thing, so do not worry about mistakes. Your journal will not be graded in any way. Your teacher will make comments on its contents only, unless you ask for the English to be corrected as well.

Points to discuss

1 Do you keep a diary? What do you put in it? What is the difference between a diary and a journal?
2 Do you feel – like many people – paralyzed when you have to start writing a composition? If so, can you explain why? How can journal writing help you to solve this problem?
3 If you let your teacher read your Journal, would you like him/her only to comment on your ideas, or to correct language mistakes as well?
4 What are the advantages of having a special Journal Book or a loose-leaf system for journal writing? Which method will you use?

Exercise 1

Now write a journal entry yourself. You can write about your first reactions (questions, objections, comments) to your reading or discussion of the above section on journal writing. Remember, journal writing is informal writing, so just write down the ideas as they come into your head.

Alternatively, you can write about a book you are reading, or a lesson or a lecture that you have just had.

Brainstorming

Brainstorming is a way of using a short burst of writing to find ideas to write about. What you do is put down on paper as fast as you can any words that come into your head in response to a cue, for example, *red, pain, evil, old friends, television, pop music*... Since at this stage you are only writing for yourself, you do not have to worry about grammar, spelling or organisation. You just jot down whatever comes into your head as it occurs to you. You can think of it as emptying your brain onto a blank page to see what you've got there!

Examples

1 You are going to read *Lord of the Flies* and as a preparation for it you are given the cue word Evil. Here is what one person wrote:

Evil – opposite of good. Catastrophes. Starvation in Africa. Just strikes out of the blue, no explanation. Suffering, mental and physical. All people are evil sometimes – cold, don't care about others – not my problem – refugees. But what if I was a refugee myself? Concentration camps, Stalin, Hitler. Torture – sadism "Man's inhumanity to Man" What makes people evil?...

There is plenty of material for a composition here, but of course it will need sorting out and organizing. That comes at a later stage. The important thing is to generate as many ideas as possible to work on.

2 In the example above the ideas mostly came out as disconnected words or phrases. But you can also brainstorm in a more organised way, as in the next example, where the cue word is Pop Music:

> I like to listen to pop music when I am doing something – like my homework or tidying my room or reading. It helps me to concentrate. It cuts out interference from outside, so I can live in my own little world. That's probably why Walkman is so popular. You can walk around with music in your ears and forget the world around you. Perhaps that's why they have music in the big stores and in restaurants and hotel lifts – wall-to-wall music – a background to make you feel good. But it does cut you off from reality as well. Another kind of pop music is at concerts, where thousands of people go mad about some group – Black Leather – playing VERY LOUD. They get sort of hypnotized by the noise and the action and the lights and the mass feelings. Pop music is more than just music.

3 Here's another form of brainstorming, on the subject "A Person I Remember from My Childhood". Here the writer collected as many candidates and reasons as possible before deciding on the best person to write about.

Mother	*Aunt Kate*
so much to say!	never married. Why? fiancé dead in war? Presents, sweets, smoked like a chimney. Football fan at 60.
Jim up the road	*Grandpa*
older, bigger, bully. Strict parents, but rich. Scared but impressed. Snow-ball fight.	lived with us – big. Big head, nose. Swore a lot. Shooting – bit head off rabbit! A real character – but what did he do? Mystery? See a man about a dog!

There seemed to be most to write about Grandpa and when the brainstormer concentrated on him, a lot of half-forgotten memories came to light. In this case a central idea also came up – "A Real Character" – to which the other memories can be related. But this will not always happen at the brainstorming stage.

Brainstorming can be an effective way of collecting ideas and developing them a little at the same time, but the risk is that you get stuck with one train of thought. There is another technique called Clustering for generating a wider range of ideas.

Clustering

Clustering or mind mapping, as it is also called, is a graphic method of brainstorming. You let your associations fan out from a central, beginning idea, which functions as the cue. Here is an example using the cue word Water:

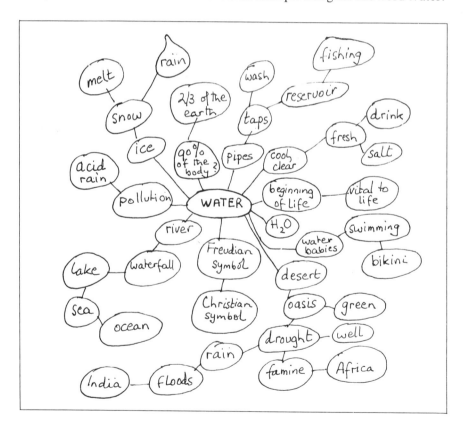

For many people this visual mode of thinking frees the mind from the logic that even sentence fragments impose, with the result that their ideas fly thick and fast from one brainwave to another. When a new thought pops up, it is easy to start again at the centre and follow the new train of associations until it runs out. Most people find, in fact, that one chain of ideas becomes so strong and leads to so many associations that they end up knowing pretty well what to write about. In the above cluster the two themes of drought and floods looked interesting, and combined with the idea of "vital to life" they led to a composition on "Water in the Third World". This meant abandoning most of the other ideas, but until you have generated them, you do not know which are the most useful ones – and which are no use at all.

Exercise 2

Practise brainstorming and clustering on any of the following cue words which appeal to you. By trying out all the methods you will find out which one works best for you.

When you have finished collecting a set of ideas, share your cluster or jottings with one or two other students. This will probably give you a few more ideas. Sharing ideas is in itself a form of brainstorming which can be very fruitful.

fashion   birthdays   sports   TV   nuclear power   spy   pop
freedom   The American Dream   exams   graffiti   vandalism

Exercise 3

Here are some more specific subjects that you can practise generating ideas on; choose one that appeals to you.

1 A Person Who Meant a Lot to Me When I Was Young
2 A Place I Remember Well
3 Something that Frightened Me
4 Something that Made Me Very Happy
5 Three Characteristics of a Person I Know Well

Interviewing

There are other ways, of course, of collecting ideas and information for a composition. Going to the library and looking up relevant articles in a book or magazine is one obvious method which professional writers use. Journalists often use interviews as well. A special kind of interview is for a Profile article – an article which presents the person who is interviewed, his or her background, work, interests and opinions. We suggest that, at the beginning of term, you write a Profile of one of the other students in your class; or why not a Profile of your teacher? You will need to interview your "victim" and take notes on what he or she tells you. Make sure to prepare some questions before you start, not only factual questions but also questions about his or her interests or opinions.

When you have done your interview, write a short Profile of about 100–200 words. You may need to go back to your victim to check what you have written or to get some missing information. Perhaps your class can make up a newsletter or wall-sheet of these Profiles so that you can all read about each other.

Exercise 4

1 Write a Profile of one of the members of your class.
2 Write a Profile of your teacher.
3 Write a Curriculum Vitae – see Appendix I, p. 119.
4 Write a short composition entitled "Woman/Man at Work". To do this you will need to observe a person at work – perhaps an assistant in the cafeteria or in the bookshop – and then interview him or her about his or her work.
5 Write about "Getting My First Job".

II Developing and Organizing Ideas

The First Draft

Let us suppose you have chosen one of the subjects in Exercise 3 to write about, for example "A Person Who Meant a Lot to Me When I Was Young". After generating some thoughts, by Brainstorming, or Clustering, or perhaps a Journal Entry, you will have chosen your person and will have some idea of what you want to say about him or her; but your thoughts will probably still be incomplete and disorganized. Or else you may have one or two ideas quite clear as starting points, but you do not yet know how to develop them.

The first draft of your composition, which you can start on now, is where you develop the ideas you have already generated, and join them up with whatever new ideas you get as you continue to write. The first step is to select and reject from the notes you have already made: "Yes, this idea is central, and it links up nicely with that one – but those don't really belong at all". "This is a good example, but I need another one", and so on. Then, as you write your first draft, you will find that you generate new ideas and again you will need to leave out some, but keep others which fit into the emerging picture.

Some lucky writers, however, will already have their ideas pretty well worked out by the time they start their first draft. In that case they can begin right away by looking for ways in which to organize their ideas: to group together ideas which belong to a common theme or argument, to find a structure for their composition.

Here are two examples of first drafts. The straightforward language mistakes have been corrected so that they do not distract from the content and organization.

A Person Who Meant a Lot to Me When I Was Young

It's difficult to know what to write about. There are quite a lot of people I could write about, but I can't think of one in particular. Maybe I should write about my teacher at school. He was great, we had great fun because he told us stories instead of teaching us history. He had a walrus moustache and swore quite a lot. Quite a character but I can't remember his name. Then there's that neighbour who never washed – but I don't want to write about her. She wasn't important. No, I think I'll write about my grandmother. She was like a mother to me, without the nagging. Because my mother went out to work, you see. She was nice, too, of course...

This example is so disorganized that it hardly deserves to be called a first draft. It wanders on as the writer jots down one idea after the other without much rhyme or reason. He is just thinking aloud, as one does when chatting to a friend – or writing a journal. But a written composition needs more discipline. The writer needs to work on a new draft in which he settles on a specific person to write about.

In the next example on the same subject you can see that there is not only a clear topic but also some kind of organisation. However, the ideas need to be developed further and more details need to be added to make it more interesting.

The most important person in my life up to the present has been a school welfare officer. I looked her up in high school, needing badly to talk to someone. To my surprise she did what few grown-ups usually do: she listened. I kept on seeing her for two and a half years, nearly every week. Talking in this way is very difficult. The situation is unnatural and so easily becomes ridiculous. Things developed slowly, not without pain. I came to know her limitations – and my own. Off and on we still meet, but do not talk only about ME. We are very good friends. She cared for me more than anyone else. But she also showed me that I am not the only pebble on the beach.

You may think that this first draft is less interesting than the first example because it does not contain as much colourful detail. But remember that the work you do on the drafts of a descriptive composition has two equally important aims: finding vivid and relevant detail to make your description come alive, and developing a clear line of thought. Only with a clear line of thought will you have a strong structure on which to build up the details of your composition.

Paragraphs

We would like to repeat how important it is that you organize your ideas into groups that belong together logically and that you have a clear line of argument – in other words that you organize your ideas into paragraphs.

A paragraph is a piece of writing about one main idea: it is a unit of thought. Often a paragraph begins with a sentence that presents the main idea – a topic sentence. You can think of the opening sentence, the topic sentence, as a kind of promise to the reader: "I am going to discuss this idea" – the idea presented in the topic sentence. So the opening sentence of a paragraph is a very important one, for both the reader and the writer. It should clearly state what is going to be discussed in that paragraph.

The following sentences of the paragraph will then develop this main idea. These supporting sentences can define or specify the idea, give examples that illustrate it or add some new information that is directly connected with it. Sentences that define and exemplify are very common components of a paragraph. Look at this example of a paragraph:

There are three qualities I most appreciate in a friend. They are honesty, humour and optimism. Of course there are other qualities I appreciate, too, like not being late and keeping promises, but honesty, humour and optimism are the most important ones for me. Without them a person could not be a true friend of mine.

The first (topic) sentence quite clearly promises to discuss three qualities in a friend. The second sentence specifies these three qualities. The third sentence gives examples of other less important examples for comparison and reiterates the three most important ones. The last sentence explains why they are so important. Presumably the three following paragraphs will in turn deal with these three qualities.

Exercise 5

Here are some opening (topic) sentences. What do you expect the paragraphs which they introduce to deal with? Which are the key words in each sentence?

Write the next sentence or two of each paragraph to show how it will develop.

1 My favourite part of Stockholm is The Old Town.
2 One of the most obvious reasons for becoming a teacher is the long holidays.
3 There are a number of very good reasons why commercial television should be allowed in Sweden.
4 There are a number of very good reasons why commercial television should not be allowed in Sweden.
5 Big city life offers many advantages.
6 There are several obvious advantages of living in the country.
7 Wish fulfilment is a very interesting psychological phenomenon.
8 Air pollution is one of the most serious threats to our environment.
9 Arguments of various kinds have been put forward against day nurseries.
10 The story of *Lord of the Flies* is quite a simple one.

In the examples above the topic sentences very clearly state – or promise – what is to come in the paragraph. Actually, a topic sentence need not always state its promise quite so obviously; and you may also decide not to make your opening sentence the topic sentence. You may, for example, want to make your reader feel curious about your topic. But at this stage we recommend you – both for your own sake and for the sake of your readers – to let your opening sentence be the topic sentence which says very clearly what you intend to write about.

We say "for your own sake" because in fact a clear opening sentence will greatly help you to keep your ideas on the right track. It is very important that a paragraph only contains ideas – and sentences – that directly relate to the main idea. Irrelevant ideas are not wanted. They will only confuse your argument – and your reader, too.

How Long is a Paragraph?

A question about paragraphing that you may have asked yourself is: "How long should a paragraph be?" The answer is that there is no standard length for a paragraph. It depends on what you have to say. Since you will have different amounts of ideas for different points, your paragraphs will be of different lengths. In fact, this is all to the good, as it gives variety to your writing, just as using both long and short words and long and short sentences does.

One word of warning: Don't copy the style of popular newspapers and advertisements which start a new paragraph with each sentence. It is very seldom that a single sentence is so important and powerful that it deserves a whole paragraph. On the contrary, the whole idea of a paragraph is that it allows the writer room to develop a topic in a logical way, and helps the reader to see what ideas in an argument go together. However, again thinking of your poor reader, you may decide that a very long paragraph of a page or so needs to be divided into two to make it more easily digestible. But – don't write one-sentence paragraphs!

We shall be returning to the question of paragraphing in Chapter III, Unity and Coherence, but we wanted to raise it now before you write a first draft as it is so important for effective writing.

Exercise 6

Write a first draft on some aspects of a subject you have explored in your Journal or you have brainstormed or clustered or in some other way collected ideas for. You could use one of the topics in Exercise 2 or 3 on page 25. You need not write more than about 100 words in one paragraph.

When you write this draft, we suggest you divide the page vertically down the middle and only write on the left- hand side. This will make it easier for you to make additions and changes on the right later. Alternatively, you can write on every other line, for the same reason. If you cannot find a word or phrase immediately, do not spend a lot of time trying to find it in a dictionary. Put in the Swedish word for the time being. It is only when you have finished your draft that you will need to look up words to find the most effective ones for your second draft. And remember, make sure that your paragraph has a clear line of argument, with a good opening topic sentence.

Response Groups

When you talk to someone, you usually get an immediate response which tells you whether what you said was understood or not. Unfortunately, this is not what happens when you write. However well you think you have expressed your ideas, you cannot be sure you will be understood; in fact, you may have expressed your ideas so unclearly that your readers do not understand what you mean.

One way to get round this problem is to read your first draft to some other people and get their reactions. Their comments and questions will help you to make your points clearer in the second draft. In the classroom it is more practical to do this response work in small groups of three or four, so that each writer gets comments from several people; but outside the classroom it may be easier for you to work with one other person, which can be just as useful. Incidentally, there are two other spin-off benefits from response work. The first is that you know you will have an audience for what you write; and the second, that you will get excellent practice in reading aloud and talking English. In fact, response group work can be great fun, as well as being very useful.

Group Work Procedure

Here is the procedure we suggest you follow for discussing a draft:

1 Each person takes it in turn to present his or her first draft.

2 Tell your group or partner what your title is.

3 Read your draft aloud to the other members of the group. Do not read too fast. Let the other members have a copy to follow in as you read and to refer to later. It is very difficult otherwise for them to make reasonable comments. As you read aloud, you may yourself discover things you want to add or change.

4 When you have finished reading your draft, each member of the response group comments on it:

　a) He gives a brief summary of what he thinks you are saying, of the main points in the draft.
　b) He comments briefly on something that he thought was successful: a convincing argument, a good example, a colourful phrase, a strong ending etc.

c) He asks one or two questions which will help the writer to see where he has not expressed his ideas clearly, or where something is missing or where something seems unnecessary. Examples of comments on the two drafts on p 28 are: "I can see your point about the difficulty of deciding on a character, but which person do you want to write about?" "Can you explain what you mean by 'Things developed slowly' – what things?" "Can you explain why you became very good friends with her?" "A specific example of what you talked about would make it clearer and more interesting."

5 The writer should not try to answer these questions - unless he does not quite understand what a question means, and needs to have it clarified. The reason for not immediately answering the questions is that this will slow down the whole response process. But note that point 6 below suggests that there may be time at the end to discuss the questions. The writer should note the questions down and any other ideas he gets from the discussion which he can use in his second draft.

6 After each writer has presented his draft and the comments and questions have been made, a general discussion may develop, especially if all the writers have written on the same subject.

You may have noticed in the procedure above that we do not mention the word criticism. We do not think that comments should consist of general value judgments like "It was boring", "I couldn't understand it at all" – or indeed of praise like "I liked that – it was super" or "Good – very good." Such general value judgments are not very useful – and in the case of negative comments they are downright depressing and counter-productive. In order to be helpful, questions and comments should be specific. Instead of "What exactly are you trying to say?" ask questions like "What do you mean by 'democratic'?" "What is your main point at the beginning?". Specific questions like these will give the writer whose ideas are still confused a chance to think about them together with a sympathetic listener. There is nothing unusual about confusion in a first draft. Confusion in the early stages is a natural part of the creative process of writing.

Here is a student's first draft. It is followed by the summaries, comments and questions which the response group members came up with.

A Problem that I Have on My Mind

I have a lot of problems on my mind nowadays. Small problems and big problems. Some problems are not even worth bothering about, but only having big problems on your mind cannot be very healthy, so I usually have a few smaller problems at the same time to make things easier.

One of my bigger problems – as I said, the small ones are not much to talk about – is what I should do with my future. What is to become of me? You might say that I have a problem that is so vast that I need to divide it up into smaller problems. But then again it is nothing worth talking about, so I will keep my dear problems to myself, as always. One should not exchange problems with others because too many problems make a very big problem.

Summaries: "It seems to me that you are telling us that you have big problems and little ones, but that you don't really want to talk about them."

"You are worried about what to do with your life, but you put that problem off by concentrating on small problems instead."

Comments: "I liked the humour, the way you are making fun of yourself and your problems."

"The way you played around with the word *problem* is nice."

Questions: "What do you mean when you say that smaller problems make things easier? An example might help – a funny one, perhaps."

"Why is it that you 'as always' want to keep big problems to yourself? Do you mean like *you* always do or like most people do? Can't you go into this a bit more?"

Exercise 7

Respond to the following first draft following the suggested procedure: summary, comments on what went well and questions. You will find a Response in the Key on p 107, but try yourselves first, in pairs or small groups.

The Second Draft

Once you have thought through the ideas of your first draft with the help of your response partners, you will be ready to write a second draft. You may find that you do not need to change very much. An example added here, a sentence moved up or down there, will perhaps solve the problems which came up in the discussion. On the other hand, you may also find – *and very many writers do* – that you need to rework your entire piece, perhaps start all over again.

What should you think about when you revise your first draft? Here are some questions to ask yourself:

1 Have I made my argument clear? Are my main points clearly developed with the help of a clear structure?
2 Is there a clear logical development between the main idea of each paragraph (the topic sentence) and the rest of the paragraph? Is there a step missing in the argument? Are there any irrelevant pieces of information?
3 What examples have I given to support my argument? Are there enough examples to make it clear and colourful?

Whether you decide that you only need to make a few changes in your first draft, or that you need a complete rewrite, it is important to realize that there is a big difference between *revising* and *editing*. When you edit, which is the last step in the writing process, you check your spelling, your grammar and your punctuation. You make sure that you have used the right word or expression, and that your sentences are complete. When you revise, however, you rework and reorganise your ideas. You cut. You add. You rearrange. You make sure that your main points are clearly stated, that every idea included is relevant to the argument; that the examples are there, and that they really do illustrate the point you intended them to. All too often people believe that a mere recopying will turn a first draft into a second or final one. This is very far from the truth. All experienced writers know that a piece of writing goes through several versions before it is ready for editing.

Example of a Revised First Draft

Let us look on the next page at a first draft and a revision of "A Grown-up Who Meant a Lot to Me". The numbers in the second draft identify the sentences which have been changed and added. As you will see, there are not many changes. Still, they develop the ideas of the first draft, they improve its clarity and they add more colour to the original version.

A Grown-up Who Meant a Lot to Me When I Was Young

The most important person in my life up to the present has been a school welfare officer. I looked her up in high school, needing badly to talk to someone. To my surprise she did what few grown-ups usually do: she listened. I kept on seeing her for two and a half years, nearly every week. Talking in this way is very difficult. The situation is unnatural and so easily becomes ridiculous. Things developed slowly, not without pain. I came to know her limitations – and my own. Off and on we still meet, but do not talk only about ME. We are very good friends. She cared for me more than anyone else. But she also showed me that I am not the only pebble on the beach.

Second Draft

The most important person in my life up to the present has been a school welfare officer. I looked her up in high school, needing badly to talk to someone. (1) She was middle-aged, with grey hair and glasses, and up to then I had thought of her as being rather stiff and formal. But to my surprise she did what few grown-ups usually do: she listened.

(2) We met nearly every week for two and a half years. (3) My development was slow, not without pain. (4) My problems seemed so hopeless, they dominated my life completely. (5) My parents had just divorced and I felt completely lost in the world. (6) I also found talking to a welfare officer very difficult, because the situation is so unnatural. (7) Instead of two equals sharing their experiences of life's difficulties, I was the poor beggar of help, while she was the giver. (8) In time, as I came to know her limitations – and my own – our relationship became more natural.

(9) Off and on we still meet, but we no longer talk only about ME. (10) I felt that she cared for me more than anyone else did; (11) but because of that care I was also able to learn that I am not the only pebble on the beach.

Exercise 8

Describe the effect of each of the above revisions. When you have completed your analysis, you can compare it with the notes provided in the Key.

Organizing the Whole Composition

So far we have been discussing mainly how you should organize a paragraph, but it is equally important that you find a structure for your whole composition. When you are writing your first draft, remember that you are looking for ideas and for a structure that will organize those ideas effectively. Concentrate on getting the main ideas together in an organized structure, with a beginning which establishes your topic, a middle which develops it and an end which draws some kind of conclusion. Do not get bogged down in details at the first draft stage. For example, if you cannot think of the English word or phrase you want to use, put down the Swedish word. You can look up the English expression later. You will almost certainly add and cut out words and phrases and reorganize your first draft as you work on it, and for this reason you need not worry too much about correctness at this stage. But it is important to remember that there is a great difference between a first draft and a final version. Never hand in a first draft as if it were a final version.

Obviously it is your ideas that should determine the overall structure of your composition, but there are a number of standard systems that you might find useful. Sometimes a chronological structure will be suitable:

Past events – Present situation – Future prospects

or an arrangement by contrasts may be best:

Advantages and Disadvantages; Arguments For and Against.

Other possibilities are:

Cause and Effect; and Problems and Solutions

Finally, it may be helpful to organize your material by listing points:

First, ... Second, ... Third, ... Lastly, ... (For an example of this arrangement, see Reasons for Journal Writing, p. 18–19).

You can also use combinations of these arrangements according to the needs of the material. Use them as a support for your ideas – not as a straitjacket!

Whatever the system you choose, it is vital that you have worked out a suitable overall organization by the time you have got on to your second draft. Otherwise both you and your reader will run the risk of losing the way in your argument.

Exercise 9 A Problem-Solving Report

You are going to write a report on a problem you personally are facing at present. The idea of this exercise is to give you a chance to apply the various ideas of the writing process in a longer composition.

Go through the following steps:

1 List all the problems you can think of that you are facing just now in, for example, your studies, your work or your private life. Jot down single words or phrases only, as you collect and generate ideas.

2 Identify the problem. Pick *one* of the problems – one that interests you particularly that you would like to write about – and formulate it in one sentence. If you like, you can begin this (topic) sentence: "The main problem I am facing in my studies/work/private life right now is...". However you formulate your sentence, it must clearly identify what you are going to discuss.

3 Response work. Exchange your sentence with another student or two and give and get comments. These comments should tell you whether your problem is expressed clearly. If necessary, change the wording of your sentence.

4 Cause(s). Now write a new topic sentence for a paragraph which deals with the cause or causes of your problem. Your sentence might quite simply begin: "The cause(s) of my problem is/are...".

5 Consequences. The next step is to describe the consequences of your problem. This sentence might begin: "The consequence(s) is/are that..." or "As a result...". As well as describing the consequences you could include any person who is affected and how bad the consequences are. Exchange sentences again.

6 Solution. Finally you will offer a solution to your problem. You might begin this sentence: "One possible solution to my problem is..." or you might like to give various alternative solutions in your own words.

7 Exchange sentences and comments with one or two students as before and if necessary rewrite any sentence that does not seem to be clear, correct or coherent.

What you have now is a skeleton composition: four topic sentences introducing four paragraphs, each of which deals with one aspect of your problem.

What you need to do next is expand, explain, define or describe in greater detail each of these aspects. They will become clearer and more interesting if you add words or phrases showing your attitude to the problem, its causes, consequences and possible solution. Find a good title for it.

Before handing in your report, check:

1 Layout: title, margin, paragraph layout.

2 Coherence: logical linking of your ideas within and between sentences.

3 Correctness: grammar, vocabulary, spelling, punctuation.

For help on these points, look at the relevant sections in Chapter V.

Finally, ask another student to respond to your report and then make any changes you feel are necessary before handing it in.

Exercise 10

Look at the Composition plan in Appendix I, p 120, and read the whole of the composition on Unemployment in Chapter IV, to see examples of overall planning. Then pick one or two of the composition subjects in Appendix II and consider what kind of overall plans might be suitable. To do this you will need to go through the stages of generating and collecting ideas and writing a first draft.

III Unity and Coherence

When you have written your first draft – or, indeed, while you are still writing it – it is very important that you think about two qualities that your writing must have: unity and coherence.

Unity means that what you write deals with one and only one main idea at a time. It is a very common mistake to bring into a paragraph irrelevant facts or ideas which, although interesting, do not have any direct bearing on the main idea of that paragraph. As we have said before, it is helpful if you begin each paragraph with the main idea, because it will then be easier for you to see what is relevant and what is irrelevant and should therefore be taken away.

Coherence means that your writing is logically developed and connected to make a clear argument. It is not enough just to have relevant ideas. You must show that they are relevant by linking them in a logical way. Let's see how far one paragraph – a piece of writing about one idea – written by a student meets the two demands of unity and coherence. The sentences are numbered for reference:

Why I Chose to Study in Grönköping

(1) There are several reasons why I chose to study in Grönköping. (2) I have a part-time job here as a hotel receptionist, which gives me a good income. (3) Most students have some sort of job because the student loans are not very good in Sweden. (4) It is not easy to live on a student loan alone. (5) My aunt has a large apartment in Grönköping where I can have a room almost rent free. (6) She is rather old but a real dear. (7) The only trouble is that she likes to talk a lot. (8) My boyfriend is studying in Grönköping. (9) He lives in a student hostel and he has almost finished his course. (10) Then he wants to work abroad for a year or so. (11) If we could find a cheap two-room flat, we could live together. (12) I have many friends who are studying at Grönköping University and I would not be happy away from them. (13) One of them has gone to the USA this year as an au-pair girl, she thinks she will learn more English that way. (14) And I think that Grönköping is a beautiful city with an exciting cultural life.

Although it is not too difficult to follow the main argument of this paragraph, it is likely that you were confused by parts of it. Some of the sentences do not seem to belong to the argument; they seem irrelevant; and it is not always easy to see how the sentences are connnected in meaning. There is a lack of coherence.

Let's look at the paragraph again in more detail. After reading the first sentence, you expect that the rest of the paragraph will give you the reasons why the writer chose to study in Grönköping. You might say that the writer gives you a promise in the first sentence: "I'll tell you the reasons why...", and this makes an excellent clear start. But how well does she keep her promise? In fact, she gives you five reasons: her job (2), her aunt's flat (5), her boyfriend (8), her friends (12) and beauty and culture (14). Scattered among these sentences, however, there are other irrelevant pieces of information which distract your attention. Her aunt's talkativeness, her boyfriend's future and her friend the au- pair girl in the US, for example, have little or nothing to do with why she chose to study in Grönköping.

These irrelevant sentences should be removed so as not to distract the reader from the main line of argument. If we do this, there will be unity of argument and the paragraph will read:

---

(1) There are several reasons why I chose to study in Grönköping. (2) I have a part-time job here as a hotel receptionist, which gives me a good income. (3) Most students have some sort of job because the student loans are not very good in Sweden. (4) My aunt has a large apartment in Grönköping where I can have a room almost rent free. (5) My boyfriend is studying in Grönköping. (6) He lives in a student hostel. (7) If we could find a cheap two-room flat, we could live together. (8) I have many friends who are studying at Grönköping University and I would not be happy away from them. (9) And I think that Grönköping is a beautiful city with an exciting cultural life.

This is an improvement because all the ideas now relate to the main idea given in the first sentence: "the reasons why". But the argument is still not very clear. The ideas are not well linked and it is difficult to see how the argument develops. But adding a few linking words (in italics in the text) will make the argument much more coherent:

---

(1) There are several reasons why I chose to study in Grönköping. (2) *First*, I have a part-time job here as a hotel receptionist, which gives me a good income. (3) Most students have some sort of job because the student loans are not very good in Sweden. (4) *Second*, my aunt has a large apartment in Grönköping where I can have a room almost rent free. (5) *Another reason is that* my boyfriend is also studying in Grönköping. (6) He lives in a student hostel. (7) *What we would really like is* to find a cheap two-room flat where we could live together. (8) I *also* have many friends who are studying at the University here and I would not be happy away from them. (9) *Finally*, I think that Grönköping is a beautiful city with an exciting cultural life. (10) It has theatres, cinemas, libraries, museums, art galleries and restaurants, apart from the university itself. (11) *Thus* it is easy to see why I chose to study in Grönköping.

We are not suggesting that this is a model piece of writing, but it does have two essential qualities which help the reader to follow its argument: it has unity and it has coherence. That is, all the sentences are relevant to the main topic of the paragraph, the reasons for choosing to study in Grönköping (unity); and the sentences are linked together in a logical way (coherence).

Unity in the Paragraph

Let us remind you of the definition of a paragraph: a paragraph is a thought unit, a group of ideas related to one main thought. A paragraph, then, consists of a series of sentences unified by *one* controlling idea or topic which is often expressed in what is called a topic sentence. It is quite common to begin the paragraph with this topic sentence, and we would advise you to do the same – even though there may in special cases be good reasons for not opening with the topic sentence. But until you feel more confident, we suggest you make the first sentence of each paragraph your topic sentence, because this will help you, the writer, to keep to the controlling topic of your paragraph. It will also tell your reader immediately what he can expect the paragraph to be about, which will help him to follow your argument. The paragraph will then continue with a number of supporting sentences. Let us look now at several different kinds of supporting sentences.

Supporting Sentences which Illustrate

Here is a paragraph written by a well-known author:

> "Every survey ever held has shown that the image of an attractive woman is the most effective advertising gimmick. She may sit astride the mudguard of a new car, or step into it ablaze with jewels; she may lie at a man's feet stroking his new socks; she may hold the petrol pump in a challenging pose, or dance through woodland glades in slow motion in all the glory of a new shampoo; whatever she does, her image sells".
> (Germaine Greer, *The Female Eunuch*)

The first sentence is the topic sentence in which the author tells the reader what to expect in the rest of the paragraph. In this case we expect to be told more about the idea that attractive women are effective in advertising. This is exactly what we get. The author gives us a few illustrations or examples of familiar advertising scenes in which beautiful women figure conspicuously. The controlling idea in the topic sentence clearly dominates the entire paragraph. A diagram might present the organisation like this:

TOPIC SENTENCE: "Every survey ever held has shown that the image of
an attractive woman is the most effective advertising
gimmick".

Sentence 2   *Supporting sentence* "she may sit ..."
Sentence 3   *Supporting sentence* "she may lie ..."
Sentence 4   *Supporting sentence* "she may hold ..."
Sentence 5   *Supporting sentence* "whatever she does ..."

Notice, too, how the writer emphasizes the parallel function of the supporting sentences by repeating "she may ...".

Sentence 10 in the last version of the paragraph about "Why I Chose to Study in Grönköping" on p. 43 is also an example of a supporting sentence that illustrates: it gives examples of the exciting cultural life of Grönköping.

Supporting Sentences which Explain

In the paragraph by Germaine Greer all the supporting sentences are illustrations or examples. But there is another very common type of supporting sentence, the sentence that explains what the topic sentence means. It may explain an unusual term, or it may explain how you intend to tackle the topic, perhaps by limiting it. Let us take a look at some examples of supporting sentences that explain.

The family has been under attack from some sociologists for several years now. And by family we mean the nuclear family of father, mother and one or more children, but no other relatives.

Here the second sentence explains the word family by defining it quite specifically. Here is another example:

> The question of compulsory national service for all young people in our country has been much debated recently. However, as this is such a vast and complicated subject, I intend to deal here with only one aspect: compulsory national service for girls. And by national service I mean a period of about one year's work in an organization that is set up by and for the state – for example, the armed forces, civil defence and certain welfare services.

The first sentence announces the topic, compulsory national service. The second sentence then limits the topic to national service for girls. And the third sentence defines the term national service.

If you feel that there is a need to define or limit your subject, it is always wise to do this right at the beginning, so that you and your reader know from the start what you are going to deal with.

Levels of Support

In the examples so far, all the supporting sentences support the topic sentence directly by giving either illustrations or explanations. However, many paragraphs have a more complex structure, with several levels of support. That is, a directly supporting sentence may in its turn have a supporting sentence. Let us take a look at another example, in rather skeleton form:

> Stockholm is a city with a high academic standing. It is the home of the University of Stockholm. It is also the home of several famous hospitals. And it is the home of the Swedish Academy.

In this skeleton paragraph the first sentence is clearly supported and illustrated by the other three sentences. In a fuller version, each of these illustrations could be expanded into separate paragraphs. For instance:

> (1) Stockholm is a city with a high academic standing. (2) It is, for example, the home of the University of Stockholm. (3) This University has one particular outstanding faculty, that of the Humanities. (4) Among its many renowned departments, the English Department is probably at the very top. (5) This Department has such well-known teachers as... (modesty forbids us to continue).

Here the diagram for the supporting sentences would look like this:

TOPIC SENTENCE: Stockholm is a city with a high academic standing.

  2 (directly supporting the topic sentence): It is the home of the
  University . . .

     3 (supporting sentence No. 2): This University has . . .

      4 (supporting sentence No. 3): Among its many . . .

       5 (supporting sentence No. 4): This Department has . . .

        . . .

As the diagram shows, only sentence No. 2 is a *directly* supporting sentence for the topic sentence. The other sentences are of a lower, and descending, order, No. 3 supporting No. 2, No. 4 supporting No. 3 and so on.

The above example has been deliberately exaggerated to show the different levels of support. In most writing, however, the various types and levels of supporting sentence are combined in more subtle ways. We suggest you study the full compositions in Chapter IV and Appendix I for more realistic examples of how paragraphs are built up.

Exercise 11

Every sentence in a paragraph should be clearly related to the main idea of the topic sentence. Take away sentences in the following paragraphs which are irrelevant to the topic sentence (in italics).

1 *There are five major political parties in Sweden.* The largest is the Social Democratic party, with almost half the seats in Parliament. In England the Labour Party is not so powerful. The Moderates or Conservatives are the next largest party with about 25% of the votes. The election system in Sweden is proportional representation. The Centre party, a non-socialist party, used to have about 25% of the votes but it is not so large today. The opinion polls give quite different results sometimes. Finally the Liberals and the Communists have about 5% of the votes each. I cannot understand why anyone votes for them.

2 *Not unexpectedly, considering the dollar exchange, many of the tourists who visited Stockholm a few years ago were American.* Then a dollar bought ten crowns worth of hotel rooms, smörgåsbord and Swedish glass, but now it is worth much less. German tourists prefer to go hiking in the mountains

or sailing in the archipelago. The largest group of tourists in Sweden, however, are the Norwegians. The Swedish economy still, in fact, benefits enormously from the fact that many of our American guests are relatively very well off. The Grand Hotel, I have been told, cannot accomodate all those who are eager to pay astronomical sums for that splendid view of the Royal Palace.

Exercise 12

Underline the topic sentences in the following paragraphs, and describe the function of the supporting sentences.

1 Have you ever wondered why English people drink so much tea? The obvious answer is that it is a cheap and harmless beverage. It is "the cup that cheers but does not inebriate". And even today you can get a good cup of tea for forty pence or so in a cafe. But these are not the only reasons for the popularity of tea. Obviously people like the taste of it, and they have very many flavours to choose from. Exotic names like Orange Pekoe Tips, Earl Grey, Darjeeling and Oolong give promise of great delight – more than just a nice cup of tea.

2 For many people nuclear power has a very threatening meaning. The words conjure up visions of the mushroom cloud of an atomic explosion, the devastation at Hiroshima, the pollution at Windscale and the disaster at Chernobyl. These reactions tend to be highly emotional but are very understandable. For nuclear power is a man-made force which theoretically could destroy civilisation on our planet, and even the planet itself.

3 In a rare instance of British overstatement, one Londoner remarked recently, "the only thing that really works in England is the theatre". To an American it is quite clear that the English theatre works because people care. To begin with, audiences care. In attending the classics, any number of playgoers arrive with the text in hand or purchase it at the theatre. Playwrights, actors and the government care. The result is variety and vitality.

4 Until the 1970's it was usually the employed mother who felt the harsh judgment of society. Because she was in the minority, she was criticized. She was put down by men and women alike, but especially by the mothers at home.

Now, however, things have changed. As more women work outside the

48

home, it is the housewives who feel that they have been left out. As working mothers receive the praise of society, the women at home feel keenly a loss of status, and with it, a loss of self-esteem. Housewives are on the defensive. For now it is Superwoman – the successful, married working mother of two – the Woman Who Could Do It All – that is the new improved image of American womanhood.

Topic Sentence Openings

The following are examples of sentence openings that can be used in formal writing to introduce a new argument. The complete sentence is then a topic sentence.

Note how different openings show, more or less strongly, different attitudes to the argument, either that you agree with the argument (Positive attitude) or that you disagree (Negative attitude) or that you neither agree nor disagree (Neutral attitude).

It is said that . . .
It is generally agreed that . . .
It must be remembered that . . .
It cannot be too strongly emphasized that . . .
It has now been proved that . . .
It is often taken for granted that . . .
It has often been questioned whether . . .
There is no doubt that . . .
It goes without saying that . . .
It stands to reason that . . .
It is easy enough (difficult/impossible) to believe (prove/argue) that . . .
It is/seems unlikely (strange/ridiculous) that . . .
It is evident (likely/obvious/possible/probable) that . . .
It is doubtful whether . . .
It would be absurd to suppose that . . .
It remains to be seen whether . . .

Exercise 13

1 Write topic sentences using appropriate openings from the list on p 49 to present the following ideas. Indicate what attitude each of your sentence conveys. For example:

A woman's place is in the home.
It is often taken for granted that a woman's place is in the home. (Negative attitude to the idea.)

1 A woman's place is in the home.
2 The car is the root of all evil in modern city life.
3 Immigrants should learn to live like us.
4 University education for all leads to a catastrophic decline in academic standards.
5 A rise in the standard of living automatically brings greater happiness.
6 Pensioners are an untapped source of knowledge and experience.
7 The attainment of equality between the sexes is merely a matter of time.
8 The Government's policy towards the developing countries is doomed to failure.
9 Nuclear power is the best answer to the world energy crisis.
10 A high rate of unemployment is inevitable in a changing society.

Note: The sentence openings listed above belong to a formal style and it would not be wise to use them to start every paragraph. The same effect of showing your attitude towards an argument can be obtained by using the attitude words and phrases listed on page 57 under 10 *Attitude*. Some of the sentence openings, but not all of them, can be replaced by these attitude words. Thus "Naturally" can replace "It is evident that . . ."; "Of course" can replace "It is generally agreed that . . ."; and "Undoubtedly" can replace "There is no doubt that . . .". However, the impersonal sentence openings have more weight and are therefore often suitable for introducing topic sentences.

2 Now add one sentence to your topic sentence to show what direction your argument will take – agreement, disagreement or neutral presentation.
3 Finally, expand your two sentences into a paragraph by giving explanations and examples to develop your argument.

Coherence in the Paragraph: Ways of Linking Ideas

As we saw in "Why I Chose to Study in Grönköping", the ideas in a paragraph need to be clearly connected and logically developed if they are to be coherent to the reader. Coherent means "hanging together, logical, organized". If ideas are not expressed coherently, they will be more or less meaningless, at least to the reader. So to show the logical connections within and between sentences, a writer needs to use various linguistic devices that signal these connections. In the next few sections we will be looking at some of these devices.

Linking within Sentences

In the right place a short, simple sentence is very effective. Too many of them in a row, however, often means that the logical connection between them is missing, as in the following example:

> Responsibility for child-care is still thought of as being the mother's. Women generally earn less than men. Their jobs are not considered important.

It is not easy to understand how the ideas of these three sentences are connected, but we can make the logical connections clear by using the conjunctions "since" and "so" to combine them into one complex sentence:

> Since women generally earn less than men, their jobs are not considered important, so responsibility for child-care is still thought of as being primarily the mother's.

Here is a list of the most common devices like "since" and "so" which are used for linking ideas *within* a complex sentence. You will certainly recognize all of them, but do you use them in your writing?

1 Simple conjunctions:	and – but – so
2 Relatives:	which – who – that, etc
3 Conjunctions: Time	when – after – before – until –
Reason:	while, etc
Condition:	because – since – as
Concession:	if – unless
	although – however (important)
4 Preposition or prepositional phrase:	After (examining the corpse)
	Before (leaving the country)
	Without (informing his superiors)
	Due to (the shortage of money)
	As a result of (breaking the law)
5 Present participle: (*-ing*-form)	Looking (at the plans, he saw that . . .)
	Being (interested I applied to join)
	A box containing . . .
6 Past participle: (*-ed* form)	Confused (by the news, he . . .)
	The methods employed (are dubious)
	This invention, introduced by . . .

Exercise 14

Now look at the following simple sentences. Link each group of sentences into one sentence, using one or more of the above linking constructions. There are usually several alternative solutions. Note that you may need to leave out some words or change the form of the verbs as well as adding link words.

1 People eat too much. People drink too much. People smoke too much. They are not very fit.
2 The Government is beginning to realize that something is wrong. It does not know what to do about it.
3 The inspector had seen all he wanted to see. He left. He did not waste any time.
4 Washington realized his mistake. He changed his plan at once.

5 It was on June 6. The Allied Forces invaded Europe. They were supported by an intense air and naval bombardment.
6 The headmaster did not want to go ahead with the plan. He wanted to hear his colleagues' opinions first.
7 There will be no chance of improving the drug situation. Society will have to change its attitudes to addicts.
8 The scheme was abandoned. It had several advantages.
9 The Government was sensitive to public opinion. It commissioned a Gallup poll.
10 The author does not present his story in the usual chronological order. He switches from past to present and back again. This is very confusing.

Suggested answers are to be found in the Key, p 109.

Exercise 15

Now rewrite the following series of sentences as a paragraph with fewer sentences. Three to five should be enough.

This is a new publicity scheme. It has not yet been tried out. It promises well. The Government is giving it its moral support. It is giving it its financial support, too. Its success will depend, of course, on its reception by the public. Their reactions are always difficult to predict. Similar schemes have been launched in the past. They have had little success. Its supporters say this: this scheme has avoided all the weaknesses of its predecessors. It is sure to be successful.

Linking between Sentences

Now that you have seen how conjunctions, relatives and participles can be used to link ideas *within* a sentence, let us go on to look at the devices used to link ideas *between* sentences. We describe three such devices: Back Reference, Sentence Order and Linking Words and Phrases.

Back Reference

The first of the devices for linking the ideas in two consecutive sentences is to use a word or phrase in the second sentence that refers back to a word or phrase in the preceding one. This back reference can be made in various ways, all of which make use of linguistic connections. Here are the commonest types:

1 Repetition of a word

The *family* is under attack. *Family* life is described as harmful.
Children and *parents* are complementary. *Children* need *parents* and *parents* provide for *children*.

Note that repetition of a word like this is not necessarily felt to be a weakness of style in English, as some people say it is in Swedish writing.

2 Replacing a noun with a pronoun

The family is still an important unit in society. *It* is not, however, identical with society.
Children are an important part of the family system. For some people *they* are the only justification for it.
Changes in the economy are the main reason for the collapse of the traditional family. *This* is not the only reason, however.

3 Using a synonym or paraphrase

The family is still an *economic* unit. *Financial* questions are still important.
The *family* used to be a self-supporting group. *Parents and children* could all work in the fields. The family provided *mutual support*; they could *help each other* in difficult times.

4 Using an antonym

The average family in Sweden used to be *poor*. Nowadays practically everyone is *rich* beyond the wildest dreams of a mediaeval lord.
At one time the family was *self-supporting*. *Now* it is highly *dependent* on the rest of society for its survival.

5 Using a comparison

Some Swedish families may complain that they are *poor*; but most families outside Western Europe and the United States are infinitely *poorer*.

6 Using an adverbial reference

The family as we know it is a product of *the late 20th century*. It was only *then* that the pattern of mother, father and only one or two children became predominant. The family system is still predominant *in most Third World countries*. *There* the family or perhaps the tribe provides the only source of support and protection.

All the above examples of coherence are based on the idea of linking by referring back to a word or words in the previous sentence. However, there will only be coherence if the reference is clear and unambiguous. Look at these examples of poor coherence:

Famine and disease decimated families in the old days. These were not improved until recently.

These could refer to *famine and disease, families* or even *the old days*, so the coherence is poor. By writing *These conditions* the ambiguity is avoided.

The father was all-powerful in most families. They gave orders to their wife and children alike.

Either *Fathers – They* or *The father – He*.

Such mistakes are not uncommon in writing, at least in first drafts. They should not occur in a finished composition.

Sentence Order

The second device for improving coherence between sentences is the order in which ideas are presented. Sometimes it is enough to put one sentence directly after another for their logical connection to be clear. (The sentences will also be linked by one or more of the types of back reference discussed above.) If the logical connection is perfectly obvious there is no need for any further linking. Most of the sentences about the family given above are of this type. Here is another example:

> When Edmund Leach attacked the family, there was an outcry from its defenders. He was felt to be striking at the very roots of society.

The second sentence of these two gives an explanation of the idea in the first sentence: it explains why there was an outcry. It is so obviously an explanation that there is no need for a linking word or phrase like "because" or "The reason was that"... (note how *roots of society* in the second sentence functions here as a paraphrase of *the family* in the first sentence).

Linking Words and Phrases

The third device, used when the connection between ideas is *not* obvious – and that means obvious to the reader – is to add a linking word or phrase which makes the connection explicit. A word of advice is necessary here: *what may seem perfectly obvious to a writer may not be obvious at all to a reader*. A writer knows which way his argument is going, but a reader is not so well informed. So, especially for an inexperienced writer, it is a good idea to make your sentence connections more explicit than you perhaps think is necessary. There is an example of this kind of explicit linking in one of the sentences about the family on p 54:

> The family is still an important unit in society. It is not, *however*, identical with society.

The linking word *however* points out that the second sentence contains an idea that contrasts with the idea in the first sentence. Other such links may point out a time relationship, a cause-effect relationship or even an attitude relationship (that is, how the writer feels about the idea in the preceding sentence).

Here are some linking words and phrases in common use. They are often placed first in a sentence, followed by a comma, to show its relationship with the preceding sentence. You can think of them as being like road signs for a car driver. They tell him in advance what is coming, thus making it easier for him to drive. In the same way linking words make life easier for the reader. As a good writer, you should make use of them.

Linking Words and Phrases

1 Time
At first
Next
Later
In the end
Eventually

2 Comparison
In comparison
In contrast
Similarly

3 Contrast
But
Still
However
Yet
Nevertheless (after a negative idea)
On the other hand (sometimes preceded by On the one hand)
On the contrary (after a negative)
In spite of this

4 Addition
Moreover
Furthermore
What is more
In addition
...also...
Nor

5 Reason
For this reason
Owing to this
...therefore...

6 Result
As a result
Consequently
So
Therefore

Thus
Accordingly

7 Order
First
In the first place
Firstly
To begin with
Second
Secondly
Lastly
Finally

8 Example
For example
For instance
Thus

9 Explanation
In other words
That is to say

10 Attitude
Naturally
Of course
Certainly
Strangely enough
Oddly enough
Luckily
Fortunately
Unfortunately
Admittedly
Undoubtedly

11 Summary
Finally
In conclusion
In short
To sum up

Exercise 16

In the following text the linking words, which are placed after the text, have been omitted. Put them back in their right places and then, in the margin, write down what type of linking device each one is.

Work expands so as to fill the time available for its completion. - - -, an elderly lady of leisure can spend an entire day in writing and dispatching a postcard to her niece at Bognor Regis. - - - a lack of real activity does not result in leisure. - - -, the thing to be done swells in importance in a direct ratio with the time to be spent.

(Heathcote Parkinson, *Parkinson's Law*)

Thus On the contrary For example

Exercise 17

In the paragraph below taken from George Orwell's essay "Politics and the English Language", the sentences have been separated and put in random order. With the help of the various linking devices he uses, you should be able to put them in the right order to make one coherent paragraph. Identify all the linking devices and explain their function; then write out the paragraph in its correct form. The preceding paragraph ends like this:

0 The defence of the English language implies more than [making pretentiousness unfashionable], and perhaps it is best to start by saying what it does not imply.

1 On the contrary, it is especially concerned with the scrapping of every word or idiom which has outworn its usefulness.

2 On the other hand, it is not concerned with fake simplicity and the attempt to make written English colloquial.

3 To begin with, it has nothing to do with archaism, with the salvaging of obsolete words and turns of speech, or with the setting up of a 'standard English' which must never be departed from.

4 What is above all needed is to let the meaning choose the word, and not the other way round.

5 Nor does it even imply in every case preferring the Saxon word to the Latin one, though it does imply using the fewest and shortest words that will cover one's meaning.

6 It has nothing to do with correct grammar and syntax, which are of no importance so long as one makes one's meaning clear, or with the avoidance of Americanisms, or with having what is called 'a good prose style'.

Exercise 18

A. Read the beginning of this student essay on "The Problems of Working Women".

A great deal has been written on the subject of working women, but there is more to be said about child-care.

One must remember that we get paid less than men, which is very unfair. Why is this so?

Responsibility for child-care is still supposed to be ours. Women generally earn less than men, so their jobs are not considered as important.

Only one third of the children of working mothers have a place in a day-nursery.

Most school-age children have no-one to look after them when they get out of school.

One must also remember that women cannot improve their status in society if they are prevented from working.

This is a situation that we must do something about.

What is wrong with this piece with regard to:

1 Paragraphing?
2 Unity?
3 Coherence?

B. Now read a rewritten version of the same piece:

A great deal has been written about the problems of working women, but there are two in particular, namely equal pay and adequate child-care, which are very important. As I shall attempt to show, these problems are related. In my opinion they are so central that true equality between the sexes cannot be said to exist until they are solved.

Since women generally earn less than men, their jobs are not considered as important, and therefore responsibility for child-care is still thought of as being primarily the mother's. In other words, when a couple have children, and no child-care can be found for them, it is nearly always the mother who gives up her job in order to stay at home with them. This means that in many areas of working life, women are just not taken as seriously as men, which is also why they are paid less.

Another reason for the inferior status of women is the shortage of day-care. For it is a fact that only one third of the children who need a place in a day-nursery get it. As for school-age children, the vast majority of those with working parents have no-one to look after them when they get home from school. As a result of this situation, many women choose part-time work so that they can be at home early in the afternoon. Of course, part-time work has a lower status on the labour market, so, once again, women are caught in the vicious circle of inequality. It seems to me, therefore, that the conditions for equality between the sexes are, first, equal value on the labour market, and second, child-care for all who want it.

Exercise 19

Now read the article below and note the ways in which the argument is connected and developed by the underlined linking words. Write down what their functions are in the margin. The first four links have been explained for you.

Are Families Necessary?

Explanations

"The family, with its narrow privacy and its tawdry secrets, is the source of all our discontent". When Edmund Leach, the Cambridge anthropologist, said *this*, there was an outcry from the defenders of the *family*. *He* was felt to be striking at the very roots of civilised society. *In fact*, Dr Leach wanted to shake us into some fresh thinking about the structure of the family in the age of working wives, the Pill and the social equality of men and women.

this refers back to the opening quotation which has clearly established the subject of the article.
family links clearly, by repetition, with the opening quotation.
The sentence order gives the implicit meaning "because he . . .". *He* refers back to Edmund Leach.
In fact introduces a contrasting explanation of Dr Leach's statements.

Even the most tenacious champions of traditional family values would admit that the intensity of family life can cause emotional disturbance from time to time. *But against this* they could point out the assistance and comfort that a family can provide when one is sick or in trouble. *Unfortunately*, families today tend to be small and widely scattered, *so that* the mutual assistance they can offer is limited. There is, *however*, an alternative to the nuclear family of children and parents living by themselves, *and this* is the extended family, represented in Britain today by the commune movement.

Of course, the idea of replacing the nuclear family unit by *a larger group* is not a new *one*. There have been religious communities in the United States since the last century and in this century we have Russian and Chinese collective farms and the Israeli kibbutzim. *The latter* communities differ from those in Britain in one essential respect. *They* are all part of the structure of society in their particular country, *whereas* in Britain the commune movement is very much anti-Establishment. Almost all communes *here* are, to a greater or lesser extent, aimed at changing the family- based structure of our society, *which* they feel is harmful to the human personality. *Certainly*, no one can deny that there are an increasing number of people who are finding the pressures of *contemporary society* too much for *them*. Problems *like* mental illness, drug addiction and alcoholism have their roots in the loneliness of *unhappy people* who cannot communicate and who feel that there is no one who cares.

The commune movement blames family life for most of *these problems*. *They* complain that the nuclear family unit is too enclosed, too isolated to be able to promote caring relationships between people. *They* claim that families just do not communicate properly with each other and that *this* leads to even more loneliness and isolation. *They* suggest that a better solution is a group of about a dozen adults, with or without

children, who all live together. *As* a
member of one commune in a London suburb said: "We aren't drop-
outs. We believe that communes can
make a real contribution to society".

Exercise 20

In the following passage from *The Autobiography of Bertrand Russell*, the
order of the paragraphs has been changed. Put the paragraphs back in the right
order with the help of the logical and linguistic signals, and analyze how they
function, both between and within the five paragraphs.

1 This has been my life. I have found it worth living, and would gladly live
it again if the chance were offered me.

2 With equal passion I have sought knowledge. I have wished to understand
the hearts of men. I have wished to know why the stars shine. And I have
tried to apprehend the Pythagorean power by which number holds sway
above the flux. A little of this, but not much, I have achieved.

3 Three passions, simple but overwhelmingly strong, have governed my life:
the longing for love, the search for knowledge, and unbearable pity for the
suffering of mankind. These passions, like great winds, have blown me
hither and thither, in a wayward course, over a deep ocean of anguish,
reaching to the very verge of despair.

4 Love and knowledge, so far as they were possible, led upward toward the
heavens. But always pity brought me back to earth. Echoes of cries of pain
reverberate in my heart. Children in famine, victims tortured by oppressors,
helpless old people a hated burden to their sons, and the whole world of
loneliness, poverty and pain make a mockery of what human life should be.
I long to alleviate the evil, but I cannot, and I too suffer.

5 I have sought love, first, because it brings ecstasy – ecstasy so great that I
would often have sacrificed all the rest of my life for a few hours of this joy.
I have sought it, next, because it relieves loneliness – that terrible loneliness
in which one shivering consciousness looks over the rim of the world into
the cold unfathomable lifeless abyss. I have sought it, finally, because in the
union of love I have seen, in a mystic miniature, the prefiguring vision of
the heaven that saints and poets have imagined. This is what I sought, and
though it might seem too good for human life, this what at last – I have found.

IV From Draft to Final Version

Summary of the Writing Process

1 *Choice of subject*: If you can choose your own subject, or between several alternatives, always write on a subject that interests you and that you know something about.

2 *Generating ideas*: Write down all the ideas on the subject that come into your head: facts, arguments, examples, comparisons, quotations, phrases, etc. Note them down in the order you think of them. Don't bother to stop and organize them. Just empty your brain onto the paper. If you have time, you can spread this idea-collecting stage over several days or even weeks. It will continue at any rate throughout all the stages of writing your composition.

3 *Limiting your subject*: You may want to limit your composition to one particular aspect of the subject, perhaps because you cannot do it justice in the time available. This is perfectly acceptable provided that you point out at the beginning of your composition how you intend to limit it.

4 *First draft*: Write your first draft. At this stage do not worry too much about correctness. That will come later.

5 *Responses*: Exchange your ideas with one or more persons, by talking about the subject with them. Read out your first draft. Tell them what you are trying to present and explain. Bring up any problems you have. As you read, you may yourself notice some improvements you can make. The responses you get will probably help you to get your ideas into perspective and generate some new ones.

6 *Organisation*: Remember that a composition both presents and explains ideas. Organise your material into groups which structure it in some kind of theme or argument. Sometimes a chronological organisation is suitable: Past History – Present Situation – Future Developments; often a contrastive organisation is fruitful: Advantages and Disadvantages or Arguments

For and Against. However you organise your material, it should have some identifiable pattern or structure. Remember, you have to help your reader follow your train of thought. Having found some sort of overall plan – it may be useful to write out this plan (see App. I, p 114) – write an organising sentence for each group of ideas. This kind of sentence which introduces a group of ideas is called a topic sentence. Note that the first sentence of your composition should identify the subject. It is not enough to refer to the title with a phrase like "This question . . .".

7 *Second draft*: With the help of the response group's comments, revise your first draft. This may involve quite substantial changes. Depending on the time available you can either present your second draft to your response group for further comments or you can go on to . . .

8 *Final version*: Go through your second draft, polishing the language. It may be necessary to make a fair copy. If your second draft is legible and well laid out, however, you need not rewrite it, though you will certainly be able to improve it by changing, adding or taking away a phrase or a word here or there.

9 *Proof read*: Check your composition very carefully for mistakes. See the check list in Chapter V.

10 Hand in your composition.

To sum up: composition writing is a *process* that takes time. Its aim is *communication*, and to achieve communication your writing needs to be *clear*, *coherent* and *correct*.

Two Examples of the Writing Process

Finally, to exemplify the writing process in use, here are two compositions which develop through the stages we have described. The first is a public debate composition on "Unemployment", the second a literature composition about Ernest Hemingway's novel *A Farewell to Arms*.

A Public Debate Composition: Unemployment

Note. In the pre-first-draft stages, Swedish words are used as stop-gaps. Looking up a lot of words in a dictionary when you are collecting material can distract you from developing good ideas. You can look them up later when you write your first draft.

Stage 1. Generating Ideas: Brainstorming

Headline news in the papers, TV, Western Europe and the USA 10–25% (arbetslöshet). In some districts even higher. Young people particularly affected. Certain industries – heavy (stål), ship-building, textiles, (gruv) and so certain districts. Car industry in America. Unemployment high among women – part time. (Förtidspensionering döljer) some unemployment.

Unemployment high in statistical terms % of (arbetsstyrka) without a (fast) job. What is the *definition* of unemployment? The working population is much larger now (?check) because of women going out to work – but kids stay at school longer. Changes in family structure and economic pressure – we need two incomes in the family.

Causes: (omstrukturering) of industry – automisation, computers, robots. Cf (jordbruk) 50 yrs ago. (Konkurrens) from the new industrial countries – Korea (S), Taiwan and from Japan. No longer (konkurrenskraftig).

Generally depressed economic situation – high rates of interest, inflation, low investment, taxes, budget (underskott), government policy, oil crisis 1973 (?) and 79. Compare situation in W. Europe with e.g. USSR – officially no unemployment there. India, Brazil – mass unemployment. Why? Same reasons?

Economic effects – private and national. Psychological - stress. Political. Cf 1930's Germany. Welfare state (lindrar) effects – unemployment benefits etc. Too little ("morot") to work? Why work? – for money
for social contact
for personal (tillfredsställelse)

Work versus leisure. Attitudes – the right to work. "Work is a four-letter word"? "Work is the curse of the drinking classes". Wilde. Something everyone is entitled to – or something that needs to be done for somebody else. (This seems to be off the subject a bit.) Teenagers' attitudes – are they different? *What will the situation be in 2000?*

Political action (fackförening – aims?) The future looks black – what ideas for helping: (delad tjänst), (arbetsförkortning), early retirement . . . (högkonjunktur) in American economy?

Stage 2. Organizing ideas

cause – effect, before – now – future
(Still seems to be too much material)

1 The situation today

What is unemployment? Different situations in different countries, industries, districts, social groups. The mass media picture – is it (vinklad ? "lies – damned lies – statistics". Relationship between working population – employed and unemployed. 15% unemployed means 85% employed. The grey economy =10%+?

2 Attitudes to work

The right to work – work – "a four-letter word". What is work for – money, social contact, personal satisfaction, a service to others? Work for the worker's sake – not for the customer. Welfare State citizen attitudes: the State (sörjer) for everyone, incl. work. Distinction between work and leisure - a modern invention of industrialism? (This section a bit irrelevant – maybe could be cut)

3 Causes of unemployment

In Western countries: restructuring industry
                     competition
                     depressed econ. sit.
                     oil crisis 73 and 79
In developing countries:
                     over-population
                     lack of industry etc
                     no functioning national economy
                     after (naturhushållning)
(This bit opens a vast new subject – better to leave it out)

4 Effects of unemployment

economic – private – national
psychological – mental stress etc
political – revolution
But the Welfare State (lindra) the effects – benefits etc.
Too many (arbetsskygga) and drop-outs? Too little (stimulans/"morot"). But a terrible situation to be (friställd).

Ways of reducing unemployment.
improved world economic situation. USA shorter working hours (30 hr week?)
job sharing
early retirement
changed attitudes to work

Yes – there's far too much here. So cut Attitudes and the international bits. Concentrate on Sweden.

Stages 3 and 4. First Draft (with comments in the margin)

1 The subject of unemployment is in the news all the time these days. This is not surprising as there are a large number of workers out of work in our country. This number is also growing, as in other countries in Western Europe and the U.S. In some districts, such as steel, mining, and ship-building, (it) unemployment can be as high as 15%. It also (drabbar) affects women and young people most. This is because so many women work part-time. Early retirement also hides unemployment. Young people have a hard time finding a job, because when work is scarce, companies do not want to spend money training beginners when they can get experienced personnel.

15% high for Sweden, has always been prosperous. Explain *why* unemployment high in these districts.

Why does part-time work lead to unemployment?

Early retirement – getting into a different subject *hidden* unemployment. Give this subject a paragraph of its own?

2 Some people have no job at all, some work part-time, but would like to work more. What percentage of the population (saknar) is without a *steady* job? It is important to define unemployment before talking about its causes. Besides, the picture presented by the media is slanted in a way. Journalists need to "sell" news by dramatizing it, and politicians have their reasons for making things seem worse than they really are. Even 15% means 85% employed. Then there is the 'grey' economy, which means that another 5% have jobs in reality, though this does not show in the statistics.

hidden unemployment again, same subject as above – put in same paragraph.

Getting into another subject – a new paragraph perhaps? But it's not really on the subject of *causes* and *effects* of unemployment. Cut.

Yes, but what do numbers mean in personal terms?
Cut this.

3 But still there *is* more real unemployment now in Sweden than 10 or 20 years ago. Some people say that the situation has not been so serious since the depression years of the 30's. Why is this so?

Not developed enough to be a paragraph.

4 One cause is the replacement of people by robots and computers as part of (rationalisering) a way of reducing costs. Machines are cheaper than human beings. Another cause is the competition from countries like Korea, Taiwan, and Japan, where both wages and taxes are much lower than here. Our prices are just too high compared with theirs.

5 Then there was the oil crisis of the 70's, which affected the whole world. Since (we) industry had to pay twice and three times as much for (oil) (bränsle) fuel, there was not enough money left over for investment. I do not know exactly how this works, but as I understand it, factories need to (tillverka) manufacture new products, and invest in new machines to improve old products, in order to keep on making money and so keep people working.

Necessary? No, everybody knows this already. Cut rest of this paragraph.

6 Our government was not prepared for the oil crisis. In fact it kept on (making new reforms) providing new public services as if the prosperity of the 60's would continue forever. The result is that we have a huge national debt.

Is this really part of the causes of unemployment?

7 The effects of unemployment are no longer starvation as in the 30's, because the state supports people in trouble. But the state cannot do anything about the mental suffering caused by unemployment. For most people, work means more than making a living. Everybody needs to feel useful. A job also gives personal contacts, and these are important in a time when the family no longer plays such a central role in society. Thus a feeling of uselessness and isolation are two important effects of unemployment, and these in turn can lead to drinking and drug problems.

This ends too suddenly.
Needs a conclusion. Perhaps a look to the future?

71

Stage 5. Final Version

The revised portions are indicated in the right-hand margin.

Explain the *effects* of the changes from the first draft.

The Causes and Effects of Unemployment in Sweden

1 The subject of unemployment is in the news all the time these days. This is not surprising as there is a large number of workers out of work in our country. This number is also growing, as in other countries in Western Europe and the U.S. *In some districts, which are wholly dependent on one depressed industry, such as steel, iron-ore mining and ship-building, unemployment has reached 15%. *This is very high by Swedish standards. We have been used to prosperity for so long that present conditions are being compared to the depression of the 30's.

*This sentence has been expanded.

*This sentence is an addition, and the next one includes an idea which in the first version came in paragraph 3 (omitted in this version).

2 Unemployment affects women and young people most. *Many women hold part-time jobs, which are the first to go in hard times. Young people have a hard time finding a job, because when work is scarce, companies do not want to spend money training beginners when they can get experienced personnel.

This subject has been given a paragraph of its own.
*This sentence has been expanded.

3 Before describing its causes, it is important to define unemployment, since much of it does not show in the statistics. Early retirement and part-time work may hide unemployment, since some people are forced to retire before they want to, and some would like to work more than part-time, but cannot find full-time jobs. The situation may, then, be even worse than that described by the official figures. What are the causes of this serious situation?

Hidden unemployment has been given a paragraph of its own. The point about slanted news in paragraph 2 of the first draft has been omitted.

4 One is the replacement of people by robots and computers as part of a way of reducing costs. Machines are cheaper than humans. Another cause is the competition from countries like Korea, Taiwan and Japan, where both wages and taxes are much lower than here. *Our prices for the products, like iron-ore, steel and ships, which gave jobs to thousands in the 50's and 60's, are just too high compared with theirs. Then there was the oil crisis of the 70's, which affected the whole world. Since industry had to pay twice and three times as much for fuel, there was not enough money left for investment.

*This sentence has been expanded in order to connect with the thought in the middle of paragraph 1.

The 'oil crisis' point has here been included in the same paragraph as the other causes, since half of paragraph 5 of the first draft has been cut. Paragraph 6 of the first draft has also been cut.

5 The effects of unemployment are no longer starvation as in the 30's, because the state supports people in trouble. But the state cannot do anything about the mental suffering caused by unemployment. First, for many people work means more than making a living. Everybody needs to feel useful. Second, a job gives personal contacts, and these are important in a time when the family no longer plays such a central role in society. Thus a feeling of usefulness and isolation are two important effects of unemployment, and these in turn can lead to drinking and drug problems.

'First' and 'second' have been added to make clear that two different effects of unemployment are being discussed.

6 What does the future hold? Automation will continue to take away many jobs. If industry cannot make profits abroad, there will be no taxes to pay for public services. The result will be more unemployment in both the private and public sectors. We must, therefore, be prepared to try new ideas, such as sharing jobs, working shorter weeks and retiring earlier. Perhaps we will no longer be able to think of a paid job as a right. The crisis of the future may require us all to change our attitudes to work.

A conclusion has been added. What is it about the conclusion that makes it a better ending than the final paragraph in the first draft?

A Literature Composition: Catherine in
A Farewell to Arms

Susanne has chosen to write a composition about Catherine in Ernest Hemingway's novel *A Farewell to Arms*. As you will see below, the ideas for this composition grew out of her journal entries. Wherever Susanne has had to use a dictionary to find the appropriate Swedish word we have included the Swedish word(s), crossed over, in the text.

We also recommend you to study the composition on *Lord of the Flies* in Appendix I, p 122.

Quotations

One very important kind of material in compositions about literature will be quotations from the text. These quotations can very effectively support your ideas and arguments if you choose and use them carefully. Look at the quotations Susanne chooses. Are they relevant to her ideas? See how she selects or rejects them as she works through her drafts, and how she uses them to support her argument.

Use the right-hand margin for your own comments on her developing composition.

Stage 1. Generating Ideas

Journal entry on the first reading of A Farewell to Arms

AFTA published in 1929 but it is still
"modern" – especially on the utnytt-
jande exploitation of women. What
a male pig Frederic Henry is! Catherine a fool. How could she let herself
be a sex-object only?

Hemingway said to have been a "pig"
himself. His view of women very
förödmjukande humiliating in the
novel.

Where is his main interest – in the war story or in the characters of F.Henry and Catherine? Is the novel a love story only perhaps?

Is the priest important? Note that F.Henry changes a lot.
I like H's style – short sentences but with a lot between the lines. Easy to read.

If I'm to write on this novel must have help in class & reread the book at least once.

Ask L. in class about themes & the main characters.

Journal entry on class discussion of A Farewell to Arms

L. defended Hemingway's attitude to women as shown in the novel. Perhaps Catherine isn't such a complete fool. Check passages in the book that perhaps can explain why she behaves the way she does.

The possible symbol of the ants falling into the fire p. 252 without Frederic doing anything to save them was interesting. I think L. exaggerated it.

Good discussion of style in first styeke paragraph of the novel and end of Ch. 30.

Catherine still idiotic to say "I want what you want" p. 84. See also several other places where she says the same, or almost the same. But see also what C. says about "rotten game" in Ch. 6.

L. pointed to interesting theme p. 193 on courage & how life kills you. Very pessimistic.

Many different opinions in class on Catherine's character.

Notes on the character of Catherine from a re-reading of the novel

First meeting of Frederic & Catherine pp. 18–20. Catherine once in love with a young soldier who died.

Second meeting (pp. 24-) F.H. tries to kiss her. She slaps him. She seems silly. F.H. in control: "seeing it all ahead like the moves in a chess game" (p. 24). She lets him kiss her.

Third meeting (pp. 27-) F.H. thinks "she was probably a little crazy" (p. 28). He is surprised at her saying "This is a rotten game we play, isn't it? (p. 28).

(They are separated; she goes to Milan, F.H. is wounded and is sent to the same hospital).

When they meet again F.H. understands he's "in love with her" (p. 74).

They become lovers & then the silly "I want what you want. There isn't any me any more" (p. 84).

"There isn't any me. I'm you" (p. 90).

"You're my religion. You're all I've got" (p. 91).

Catherine becomes pregnant. Afraid F.H. is angry (p. 110). He says

"You always feel trapped biologically" (p. 110). Note – there is a place later in novel where this is repeated.

F.H. thinks C. brave (p. 110).

"I am a simple girl" (p. 121). (How true!)

What to make of Marvell's poem p. 122?

Probably central passage p. 193 on Catherine and courage "If people bring so much courage to this world the world has to kill them to break them ..." (p. 193). (See also later in novel on people being "broken" – where?

They flee to Switzerland. Happy (p. 216).

Talk about marriage p. 225. Still Catherine silly about being alone pp. 229, 231.

Hospital to give birth p. 245. "This was the end of the trap" – cf. above p. 110.

Catherine feels "broken" p. 248. Cf. note above from p. 193.

Catherine dies – is stoic before death p. 225.

Stage 2. First Draft

The paragraphs are lettered for easy reference. Write your comments on the draft on the right.

The Character of Catherine in AFTA

a Hemingway is said to have had rather old-fashioned views about women. At least his views seem old-fashioned to-day. I remember pictures of him as a hunter, with "tough" clothes, a big rifle etc – the typical "tough" male out to hunt animals and women, no doubt. When such a man writes about women it is not surprising if the women are treated as sex objects.

b This is what happens in *A Farewell to Arms*. Catherine is described as a complete fool in the beginning. She doesn't want Frederic to kiss her but after a little while she doesn't mind it at all. Frederic can control the whole situation "like the moves in a chess game" (p. 24). He understands that she "was probably a little crazy" (p. 27) but he thought that was o.k. He decided to treat her, or rather his förförelse seduction of her like a "game, like bridge" (p. 28). The only time he is surprised is when she says "This is a rotten game we play, isn't it?" (p. 28).

c Nevertheless, when he hasn't seen her for a while he misses her. And when they meet again in Milan, in the hospital, he realizes for the first time that he is in love with her (p. 74).

79

d Her silliness is shown clearly after they have become lovers. All she can think of is that Frederic is the most important thing in the world to her: "I want what you want. There isn't any me any more" (p. 84; cf. also p. 90). She even thinks that Frederic is as important as religion (p. 91). And she is always afraid that he will get tired of her or that she will be a nuisance to him. She doesn't want him to feel trapped by her when she has become pregnant (p. 110). She thinks, rightly, that she is a "simple girl" (p. 121).

e Frederic seems to feel highly about Catherine in a passage where he praises her courage:

> If people bring so much courage to this world, the world has to kill them, to break them, so of course it kills them. The world breaks every one and afterward many are strong at the broken places. But those that will not break it kills. It kills the very good and the very gentle and the very brave impartially. If you are none of these you can be sure it will kill you too but there will be no special hurry (p. 193).

f At the end of the novel Catherine feels "broken" (p.248) when they understand that "This was the end of the Trap" (p. 245). But she shows great courage. She tries to comfort Frederic not long before she dies in childbirth. And Frederic is very sad when he walks away in the rain all alone in the world.

Stage 3. Response Group

The first draft is read to, and by, a response group of three classmates, Anne, Christina and Magnus. You will find a selection of their comments and questions on each paragraph in the right-hand margin. (Don't expect all comments to be equally helpful – they never are.)

a Hemingway is said to have had rather old-fashioned views about women. At least his views seem old-fashioned to-day. I remember pictures of him as a hunter, with "tough" clothes, a big rifle etc – the typical "tough" male out to hunt animals and women, no doubt. When such a man writes about women it is not surprising if the women are treated as sex objects.

Anne: Why do you tell us about Hemingway's own views? And what does his hunting have to do with Catherine? I kind of like your last sentence though.
Christina: I think you should cross out the first paragraph altogether. Begin to discuss Catherine right away.
Magnus: I think it's interesting to get to know a little about Hemingway. I think you should keep it. I like his views of women.

b This is what happens in *A Farewell to Arms*. Catherine is described as a complete fool in the beginning. She doesn't want Frederic to kiss her but after a little while she doesn't mind it all. Frederic can control the whole situation "like the moves in a chess game" (p. 24). He understands that she "was probably a little crazy" (p. 27) but he thought that was o.k. He decided to treat her, or rather his förförelse seduction of her like a "game, like bridge" (p. 28). The

A: Is Frederic right in having so low an opinion of Catherine? What do you think Catherine means when she talks about "this rotten game"?
C: Yes, I think you could write more about the situation where Catherine shows that she knows what Frederic wants.
M: I like it the way it is.

81

only time he is surprised is when she says "This is a rotten game we play, isn't it?" (p. 28).

c Nevertheless, when he hasn't seen her for a while he misses her. And when they meet again in Milan, in the hospital, he realizcs for the first time that he is in love with her (p. 74).

A: Does this tell us anything about Catherine's character? I think you show too much interest in Frederic here.

C: I think you could leave this paragraph out.

M: Frederic said he had missed her earlier, but how could he know so suddenly that he loved her?

d Her silliness is shown clearly after they have become lovers. All she can think of is that Frederic is the most important thing in the world to her: "I want what you want. There isn't any me any more" (p. 84; cf. also p. 90). She even thinks that Frederic is as important as religion (p. 91). And she is always afraid that he will get tired of her or that she will be a nuisance to him. She doesn't want him to feel trapped by her when she has become pregnant (p. 110). She thinks, rightly, that she is a "simple girl" (p. 121).

A: In the passage you quote from p. 84, I think Catherine shows she is a very unselfish person. Perhaps she exaggerates it because she wasn't very kind to the boy who died – the one she was going to marry, I mean.

C: Yes, Anne is right, I think. Catherine seems to feel guilty about the way she treated him.

M: Catherine is a "simple" girl all right. Nice to have a girl like that. How about a connection between what she says about being "trapped" p. 110 and what you quote later: "this is the end of the trap"?

e Frederic seems to feel highly about Catherine in a passage where he praises her courage:

> If people bring so much courage to this world, the world has to kill them to break them, so of course it kills them. The world breaks every one and

A: Why do you think Hemingway has Frederic say this and not Catherine? And why do you quote the passage here?

C: I think this may be *the* central passage in the novel – wasn't that what L. said? One of the central ones anyway. Perhaps you could get more out of this?

afterward many are strong at the broken places. But those that will not break it kills. It kills the very good and the very gentle and the very brave impartially. If you are none of these you can be sure it will kill you too but there will be no special hurry (p. 193).

M: How can Frederic know here that Catherine is so brave? She hasn't done much so far in the novel, has she?

f At the end of the novel Catherine feels "broken" (p. 248) when they understand that "This was the end of the trap" (p. 245). But she shows great courage. She tries to comfort Frederic not long before she dies in childbirth. And Frederic is very sad when he walks away in the rain all alone in the world.

A: Catherine shows courage here that's true, but do you mean that she feels "broken" *because* of a kind of "trap". I don't understand this.
C: I agree with what you say here but shouldn't you try to have some kind of a conclusion?
M: I like the ending with the rain. Like "Singing in the Rain" – only crying.

Stage 4. Second Draft

Susanne has revised her first draft with the help of some of the comments and questions from her response group. Her second draft is given below. This is the first version that her teacher, L. reads. His comments on the draft are found in the right-hand margin, where you should try to analyze the changes between the first and second drafts.

a When we first meet Catherine she appears to be a complete fool, at least when it comes to her relationship with men. Frederic concludes she is "probably a little crazy" (p. 27) after she has first refused his kiss, then has let him kiss her, and already at their third meeting having exclaimed "I love you so and it's been awful" (p. 27). Frederic knows he is in control of the situ-

Quite true, Catherine appears to be foolish because we see her through Fredric's eyes.

ation, which he sees "like the moves in a chess game" (p. 24). Using another comparison, he describes his plan for seducing Catherine as if he were to play a "game, like bridge" p. 28). He is surprised, however, when he finds out that she understands the rules of the game perhaps as well as he does. He is rather shocked at hearing her say "This is a rotten game we play, isn't it?" (p. 28).

Hemingway corrects our impression of her soon though, doesn't he? I mean the line which you have yourself drawn attention to: "This is a rotten game ..." Perhaps you could emphasize this contrast more?

You focus a little too much on Frederic; shift to Catherine.

b Once Catherine and Frederic have become lovers, she seems to want to lose her own identity: "I want what you want. There isn't any me any more" (p. 90). From now on she only thinks of Frederic's wishes and desires, even sexual ones; when she has become pregnant, she's afraid Frederic will get tired of her. She wants to please him in everything.

c Perhaps Catherine's självutplå-nande self-effacing behaviour can be explained by her experience with the boy she was going to marry the year before she met Frederic. She had known him for eight years, but he was killed before they could marry. Maybe she felt guilty about her treatment of her first fiancé.

A possible psychological explanation —perhaps it should be developed further.

Relevance of this sentence (as now written) not clear to me. Develop or scrap it.

You're on to something here; look for further evidence in the novel and develop.

d Frederic's opinion of Catherine becomes more and more positive as time passes. With her he never feels lonely the way he has felt when making love to other girls. But it wasn't just in the night when they made love that he felt like that. He

Again you focus too much on Frederic —your starting point should be Catherine's character.

felt close to her all the time and it seems as if it was Catherine's great courage that made him feel like this. For just after he has thought about his sense of ~~kroppslig och andlig gemenskap~~ physical and spiritual affinity with Catherine he praises her courage:

> If people bring so much courage to this world, the world has to kill them, so of course it kills them. The world breaks every one and afterward many are strong at the broken places. But those that will not break it kills. It kills the very good and the very gentle and the very brave impartially. If you are none of these you can be sure it will kill you too but there will be no special hurry (p. 193).

Good passage to bring in, since it conveys one of the main themes of the novel —as we discussed it in class. Perhaps you could emphasize C's role in the novel in relation to this theme still more?

e At the end of the novel Hemingway dramatizes the "truth" of Frederic's reflection. Catherine has been very brave throughout their relationship and is so now as she expects to die. She, too, at this moment understands that people get broken, as she admits that "I'm all broken. They've broken me. I know it now" (p. 248). Therefore, her experience, like Frederic's, seems to prove to Frederic that they were trapped. Early in the novel he said that "you always feel trapped biologically" (p. 110) and at the end he can conclude: "This was the end of the trap" (p. 245).

Your final paragraph is all true and it's fine that you have noticed the two references to the idea of being trapped, but this is not a satisfactory ending to an essay on Catherine's character.

Generally, you have the materials of a fine essay here. Now focus on C. & develop the ideas you've got around a clearly stated thesis— a central point you wish to make about her. Have you made an outline for your essay?

Summary of criticisms from teacher

1 Focus on one central line of argument, a *thesis* for the essay.
2 Focus on Catherine, not on Frederic.
3 See what can be made of C's experience with her dead boyfriend. Find evidence – re-read certain passages.

(Your teacher may accept your second draft with only minor changes as your final essay; but it is likely that (s)he will suggest some changes – perhaps only a few points, perhaps of the whole structure of your essay. In both cases you will need to write a final version and edit it carefully for language mistakes.)

Outline Plan for the Final Version

Thesis: Hemingway treats Catherine as a tragic heroine worthy of our respect and sympathy.

    a Introduction (Different versions of Catherine; my three main reasons for thinking H. wants the reader to admire C.)
    b Frederic's sudden change of opinion about C.
    c C's experience with her first boyfriend.
    d C's courage.
    e Conclusion?

Stage 5. Final Version

Catherine in A Farewell to Arms

a Many readers of *A Farewell to Arms* find Catherine a very silly woman, and she is often taken as an example of Hemingway's notoriously male chauvinist opinion of women. There are certainly passages in the novel which can be used to support this view. However, there are three main reasons why I think Hemingway wants us to respect Catherine. Firstly, he makes Frederic change his opinion of Catherine quite suddenly at the beginning of the novel. Secondly, he seems to suggest that her behaviour towards Frederic to some extent is the result of her feelings of guilt after her experience with her first boyfriend. And thirdly, he emphasizes her courage to such an extent that her story illustrates one of the main themes of the novel.

A fine introduction Susanne: you state your thesis clearly — and it's a sensible one!

b Our first impression of Catherine is through Frederic's eyes. To him, Catherine doesn't seem very bright. In fact, he suspects that she is "probably a little crazy" (p. 27). As he soon finds out, however, this is a very mistaken view of her. For, in the middle of his planning of how to seduce her – a process which he looks upon as a "game, like bridge" (p. 28) – she suddenly surprises, and embarrasses, him by saying "This is a rotten game we play, isn't it?" (p. 28). She makes it very clear to Frederic, and to the reader, that she understands the rules of the game just as well as he does, and that she will not be a simple plaything for him.

Good! The focus is now on Catherine.

c From then onwards, Catherine's behaviour towards Frederic can probably be explained by her tragic experience with her first boyfriend. He was killed without, it would seem, her having allowed him to make love to her, despite the fact that they had known each other for eight years. She now regrets this very much "I was a fool not to [marry him]. I could have given him that anyway . . . He could have had anything he wanted if I had known" (p. 19). Obviously she very much regrets her treatment of him, and perhaps it is this guilt that makes her exaggerate her devotion to Frederic. Seen in this light, even her extreme wish to lose her own identity seems less extravagant: "I want what you want. There isn't any me any more" (p. 90). This ← *good point* almost seems like a conscious sacrifice of herself for the sake of Frederic's happiness – or perhaps a punishment for what she thinks of ← *self-inflicted punishment, you mean?* as her cruel and selfish attitude towards her boyfriend.

d Whether she thinks of it as a sacrifice or a punishment, Catherine *successful transition* enters her relationship with Frederic ~~utan hänsyn~~ till regardless of the consequences and showing great courage. In fact it is Catherine's courage which seems the basis of Frederic's sense of a closer physical and spiritual affinity with her than with any woman he has ever known (see pp. 191–193). And it is perhaps in Frederic's emphasis on Catherine's courage that we find the clearest evidence of Hemingway's high opinion of her:

> If people bring so much courage to this world, the world has to kill them <u>or</u> break them, so /to *be careful with quotations* of course it kills them. The world breaks every one and afterward many are strong at

the broken places. But those that will not break it kills. It kills the very good and the very gentle and the very brave impartially. If you are none of these you can be sure it will kill you too but there will be no special hurry" (p. 193).

Thus I wish to argue that Hemingway suggests that the "truth" of what Frederic is saying here is shown in what happens to Catherine. There is even an echo of the passage late in the novel as Catherine understands she is going to die: "I'm all broken. They've broken me. I know it now" (p. 248). The fact that she is broken makes her an admirable character in this context: she is broken exactly because she has the kind of courage that Frederic has mentioned, the kind it takes to make a character tragic and heroic.

You have been wise not to attempt a separate conclusion in this case: you explain your three reasons in three separate paragraphs clearly & convincingly — no conclusion is necessary in these circumstances.

A fine essay, Susanne!
L.

V Editing

Layout

In order to help the reader to follow your argument, you should lay out your composition like this:

1 Title: Write the title at the top of the first page and underline it. If you are using a word processor, you can write the title *in italics*.

2 Opening sentence: Normally the first sentence of your composition should identify the subject. It is not enough to refer to the title with a phrase like "This question . . .". It is often a good idea to use the key words of the title in the first sentence.

3 Margin: Leave a broad margin – at least 5 cms – on the left-hand side of each page.

4 Paragraphing: Start each new paragraph with a clear indentation. Look at any typed or printed piece of English to see how paragraphs are laid out. If you are writing by hand, we also recommend you to leave a double space between paragraphs.

As you know, a paragraph is a piece of writing that expresses one main idea; it often starts with a sentence that presents this idea (the topic sentence) and continues with a number of other sentences that expand and illustrate the idea. Consequently, the one-sentence paragraph is rare indeed. Such a stray sentence usually belongs to one of the other paragraphs or needs to be expanded into a longer paragraph. In contrast, a composition that consists of only one long paragraph is also likely to need revising. It will be difficult for your reader to see how your argument develops unless you divide it up into logical steps in the form of separate paragraphs with clear connecting links.

The Appropriate Style: Formal and Informal

Certain words and phrases commonly used in informal (colloquial) speech and writing are not appropriate to formal written English. If you look at some examples of formal written English, quality newspapers and text books, for example, you will see what the modern usage is.

In your formal compositions you should avoid the informal style given in the left-hand column and instead use the formal style given in the right-hand column.

Informal	*Formal*
1 Short verb forms: they're, he'd, can't, won't etc.	Use the full verb forms: *they are, he would, cannot, will not* etc. Note: *cannot* is one word.
2 Abbreviations: e.g., i.e., etc.	Do not use abbreviations; use *for example, that is, and so on.*
3 Have got/Has got	Use *Have/Has* alone without *got.*
4 A lot/Lots of	Use *A great many/A good many* with countable nouns; *A great deal of/A good deal of* with uncountable nouns.
5 You (in the sense of Sw.'man')	Use *We, They, People, One* according to the meaning; or an Impersonal construction; or a Passive construction.
6 Nice (a vague and rather meaningless word)	Find a more exact word: attractive, advantageous...
7 Thing (another vague and rather meaningless word)	Find a more exact word; or reword the phrase to avoid *thing: What is most interesting is...*
8 Conversational opening phrases: Well, You see, Yes...	Leave them out.

9 I think ... (in particular at the beginning of a sentence)	Leave it out; or use it inside the sentence: *"This problem is, I think, the most serious one"*.
10 This (= Detta, used alone to refer to a previous idea.)	To clarify the meaning you will probably need to add a word: *This problem, This situation, This argument* etc.
11 Question and answer, as in a dialogue. For example: "What are the advantages of this scheme? It is not easy to answer this question".	Occasionally a rhetorical question may be an effective way of catching your reader's attention, but often it is better to combine the question and answer in a statement: *It is not easy to see the advantages of this scheme.*

Stylistic Devices

There is one side of writing which we have not mentioned so far: stylistic devices. These are the ways in which a writer chooses and arranges words to create special effects. This is such an enormous and complex subject that we cannot do more than touch on one aspect of it here: the sound quality of what you write. Even when words are written down, they still keep their sound qualities, which the reader, consciously or unconsciously, will absorb. So it can be effective to use devices like alliteration – the repetition of the same sound at the beginning of words, for example "pride and prejudice", "the triumph of mind over matter", or "ladies of leisure". These echo effects give a ring to your writing which makes it more memorable and therefore more effective.

Another effective device of the same kind is the use of balanced phrases, either in pairs – "pride and prejudice", for example – or in threes – "blood, sweat and tears", "Father, Son and Holy Ghost", "faith, hope and charity", for example. Here it is the rhythmic effect that these balanced phrases give to writing that can be both pleasing and persuasive (another example of the same device). Other well-known examples of three-grouping are: "yesterday, today and tomorrow", "He was tall, dark and handsome" and "I came, I saw, I conquered". These phrases are clichés – well-worn phrases – but usually you will need to make your own groups to illustrate the ideas you are presenting.

For example, a composition on "Pollution" might say, of loud traffic noise, that it is "harmful, unpleasant and unnecessary", or even better "unhealthy, unpleasant and unnecessary". Why is this an improvement on the first attempt?

Of course, it is not enough for the two or three items that you group together to belong together logically and to sound good. They must also match each other grammatically. Thus you can group two or three verbs together, or nouns or adjectives, but you must not mix nouns, verbs and adjectives in the same group, like this: "The problem is a mess, insoluble and cannot be tackled nationally". Even if the ideas belong together, the lack of grammatical balance – noun + adjective + verb phrase – spoils the rhythmic effect.

We suggest that you keep your eyes – and ears – open for examples of stylistic devices like alliteration and balanced phrases (sometimes called parallelism), in the books you read. You will find several examples on pages 112–115 in the introduction to Bertrand Russell's *Autobiography* and "Are Families Necessary". Gradually you yourself will learn to "play" with words and phrases when you write, so that your sentences will not only be clear, correct and coherent but also have a satisfying rhythmic ring to them.

Punctuation

The Comma

The comma has slightly different uses in Swedish and English. Here are a few guidelines and examples.

1 Do *not* use a comma before *that*.

  a *That* can introduce an object clause after a verb:

    He pointed out that the answer was wrong.
    The committee decided that the meeting should be postponed.

  Note that words like *why* and *where* can also introduce an object clause without a comma.

b *That* can also introduce a defining clause (*nödvändig sats*):

The doctor that treated me was Dr Soames.
The present that she liked best was the diamond ring.
She gave all that she owned to the poor.

2 Defining clauses can also be introduced by '*which*', '*who*', '*where*', etc, but should still not have a comma:

I bet on the horse which came last.
We met the man who lives next door.
Liverpool is the town where the Beatles were born.

3 A comma *is* used before non-defining clauses (*icke-nödvändiga satser*):

We met Mr Brown, who was looking very pleased with himself.
Pride and Prejudice, which was written before 1800, was not published until 1813.
She is from Brazil, where the nuts come from.

Defining and Non-defining Clauses

The function of a defining clause is to identify, to define the person or thing you are writing about. If you leave out a defining clause, the sentence loses or changes its meaning. A non-defining clause just adds a piece of information that is not vital to the sentence. If it is left out, the sentence still stands and will have the same basic meaning. In fact, the commas round a non-defining clause represent the pauses and changes in intonation you make when you say the sentence.

Sometimes it may be difficult to decide whether you want a clause to be defining or non-defining, but more often the difference is highly important and the commas are therefore vital to the meaning of what you write. Look at these examples:

All the workers, who were on strike, were sacked.
(All the workers were sacked.)

All the workers who were on strike were sacked.
(Only the workers who were on strike were sacked.)

My wife, who is in New York, returns tomorrow.
(Only one wife)

My wife who is in New York returns tomorrow.
(Trouble ahead. He has another wife somewhere else.)

4 A comma is used before *which* with the meaning *and this (vilket)*:

The manager refused to negotiate, which made a strike inevitable.
Most of the students have passed their exams, which is very encouraging.

5 A comma is used before and after words in apposition to a previous word:

Mrs Thatcher, the British Prime Minister, visited Berlin.
Then came the sequel, *Life at the Top*, a much less interesting novel.

6 A comma is used before and after sentence adverbs when they are inside a sentence and after them when they come first in a sentence:

This, however, was only the beginning.
The result was, in fact, quite the opposite.
Nevertheless, the problem was solved.
Actually, the damage was less than had been feared.

7 When a sub-clause (*bisats*) comes before a main clause (*huvudsats*), a comma is often used between the two clauses; do not use a comma when the main clause comes first:

When the war was over, the troubles began.
If there were fewer cars, there would be less pollution.
Teenagers behave like this because they have no alternative.
Golding changed the opening chapter of *Lord of the Flies* quite radically before the novel was published.

The Semi-colon

8 A semi-colon is often used where there is a clear logical connection between the two sentences, though they are still grammatically separate. In fact, as you will see from the examples below, there is often a choice between using a full stop, a conjunction linking the ideas or a semi-colon. The important thing is to use at least a semi-colon (or a full stop, or a conjunction) and not a comma between two main clauses. Here are a few examples using the semi-colon:

Unemployment continues to be a serious problem; in some parts of Britain it is above 20 per cent.

Hamlet is a man paralysed by his own conscience; he cannot bring himself to avenge his murdered father by killing the king.

Half the fun of writing is the way it helps you to think; it is only when you have written down an argument that you can see whether it really holds water or not.

Some people never use a semi-colon; personally I find it a very useful mark of punctuation, half way between a comma and a full stop.

Run-on Sentences

9 Do not write run-on sentences. A run-on sentence is two or more sentences that have wrongly been put together as one sentence. Here are some examples of run-on sentences:

> Commercial television has a part to play in Sweden, it can lead to better programmes. (Wrong)
> Simon is a fascinating character, he represents the mystical side of human nature. (Wrong)
> Only one thing about town life is entirely bad and that is the pollution, it cannot have any advantages. (Wrong)
> She had a way of trying to forget what had happened, she could not stand reality. (Wrong)

Instead of using a comma to link the sentences above, you should use one of the following alternatives:

a Put a full stop between the sentences:

> Commercial television has a part to play in Sweden. It can lead to better programmes.
> Only one thing is entirely bad about town life and that is the pollution. It cannot have any advantages.

b Put a conjunction between the two sentences to show the logical connection:

> Simon is a fascinating character because he represents the mystical side of human nature.
> She had a way of trying to forget what had happened since she could not stand reality.

c Put a semi-colon between the two sentences:

Simon is a fascinating character; he represents the mystical side of human nature.

Only one thing about town life is entirely bad and that is the pollution; it cannot have any advantages.

Incomplete Sentences

10 Do not write incomplete sentences, that is, sentences without a main clause. Here are two examples of incomplete sentences:

When he was treated as a person, Dibs acted like a normal child. Like when he was with his grandparents. (Wrong, no main clause in the last "sentence")

Many single parents leave their babies in day nurseries for the whole day. Because they cannot afford to work part-time. (Wrong)

The easiest solution to this mistake is to use a comma instead of a full stop:

When he was treated as a person, Dibs acted like a normal child, like when he was with his grandparents.

Another solution is to make the incomplete sentence into a proper sentence:

Many single parents leave their babies in day nurseries for the whole day. The reason is that they cannot afford to work part-time.

Advertisements and newspaper articles sometimes use incomplete sentences, but this is to give a special, pseudodramatic effect; they are not usually acceptable in formal essays.

The Colon

11 A colon is used to introduce lists and quotations:

Australia's chief exports are: wool, wheat, coal, uranium and precious metals.
As Hamlet says: "To be or not to be: that is the question".

Remember that the main function of punctuation is to help your reader to follow what you are saying. It corresponds to some extent to the pauses, intonation patterns and even gestures that you use when talking. Punctuation is partly a personal matter and there are very few absolute rules governing its use; we suggest you look at the way the texts in this book are punctuated for further guidance.

A useful handbook on punctuation is *Mind Your Stop*, G.V. Carey, Pelican.

You will also find some useful rules and examples in Svartvik-Sager, *Engelsk Universitetsgrammatik*, pp. 440–42.

Exercise 21

Put in the missing punctuation marks where appropriate:

1 Canterbury which dates back to Roman times has recently become a university town.
2 One of the English towns which have Roman connections is Canterbury.
3 Rosemary who was still at school was not expected home until later.
4 He had two children who were still at school and one who was at univeristy.
5 It was none other than Benjamin Franklin who decided Thomas Paine's future for him.
6 *The Way of All Flesh* which was not published until after Samuel Butler's death is an autobiographical novel.
7 He agreed to my suggestion which surprised me very much.
8 The library did not have the book which I wanted and which they had promised to get for me.
9 The Minister assured them that there was no risk involved.
10 The committee wishes to point out that it does not approve of the scheme.
11 There is no doubt that the figures are correct.
12 They could not give one good reason why they should stay.
13 The last suggestion is in fact the most feasible.
14 Charlie Chaplin the famous comedian wrote his autobiography late in life.
15 Darwin's contemporaries however were shocked by his theories.
16 Sweden like Britain sought entry to the Common Market.
17 At first sight no doubt these statistics look impressive.
18 If as we suspect the decision was based on false premises we must do our best to reverse it.
19 A great deal of damage was done by the fire before it could be brought under control.

20 Unfortunately most of the building was damaged by water.
21 However the chapel was saved.
22 When they left the children remembered to thank their host.
23 That was the position when William the Conqueror landed at Pevensey Bay.
24 Since he ran the risk of being charged with treason Buckingham fled to France.
25 Lady Jane refused all offers to go into films although her sister Lady Bird is an actress at present appearing in a play in the West End.
26 The candidate did not give a good impression he looked as though he needed a shave.
27 It was difficult to persuade them to leave they insisted on staying to the bitter end.
28 This is my advice Don't.
29 Sweden won several medals one gold two silvers and five bronzes.
30 The fact that Amerigo Vespucci a comparatively unknown Florentine was the man who gave his name to the only continent that has been called after a person has however often been quoted as an example of historical injustice.

Spelling

Make sure you can spell the words in italics. Study them carefully and check your spelling by writing them out from memory.

1 It is not easy *being* a student.
2 I shall *choose* the same as I *chose* yesterday. This is my *choice*.
3 I do not want to *lose* my *loose* tooth.
4 She *says* the same as she *said* yesterday.
5 He was *quite quiet*.
6 These *two* are *too* good *to* be true.
7 *It's* time to give the dog *its* food.
8 *Their* bags are *there*.
9 *Which witch* did you see?
10 It is doubtful *whether* the *weather* will be good enough.
11 *Where were* they last night?
12 *Who's* got *whose* book?

1 Modern *British literature*, by *Professor* Smith, a *colleague* of mine.

2 I was *dying* with *embarrassment*, but I never *died*.

3 They gained *peace* in return for a *piece* of land.

4 I am *extremely grateful* for your *great* help.

5 That was the *advice* I *received*. Who *advised* you?

6 What was the *price* they *paid* for the *prize*?

7 *Queues* are *unnecessary*.

8 The *physical* and *psychological development* was phenomenal when it *occurred*.

9 The *pronunciation practice* was wholly *successful*. They *succeeded* by *practising pronouncing* difficult words every day.

10 They *seized* and now *possess* a *beautiful* but *underdeveloped* island.

11 The *whole* project was a *catastrophe*

12 Of *course* he was *disappointed* by his *friend's disappearance*, and not without *cause*.

13 *Chemistry* and *physics* are *parallel* subjects.

14 The *effects* of the accident did not *affect* his *judgment/judgement*.

15 *Rhythm* and *rhyme*.

16 He *speaks* well when he makes a *speech*.

17 If the *brakes break*, the car will crash.

If you cannot spell a word, write it out ten times or so, and try to see a picture of it in your mind's eye.

Capital Letters

English uses capital letters at the beginning of words more than Swedish does:

Person's Titles: The Prime Minister, Mrs Thatcher, Sir Arthur Conan Doyle, Lord Peter Wimsey, Professor Smith, etc.

Book Titles, etc.: Lord of the Flies, Gone with the Wind, A Farewell to Arms, News at Ten, etc.

As you can see, the small words in titles are not capitalized.

Nationality words: British, English, Swedish, Japanese, etc.

Date Words: Monday, Tuesday, January, February, Christmas, New Year's Eve, Easter, etc.

The Apostrophe s

1 -'s with singular nouns:

Hemingway's attitude to women
Their only son's future
The Government's policy

2 -s' with plural nouns ending in s:

His parents' house
All the countries' votes
Five weeks' holiday

3 -s' or -'s with names that end in s:

St. James's Square
The Jones's house/ the Jones' house
Charles Dickens' novels
Socrates' philosophy

There seems to be no fixed rule for names that end in s.

4 's for decades:

In the 60's/60s/sixties
The 1930's/1930s/thirties

The forms without an apostrophe are very common.

5 In short forms of verbs:

There's no doubt
I don't know
It's difficult to say

These short forms are only used in informal writing.

NOTE The form it's = it is. The pronoun *its*, for example in *The Government and its policies*, never has an apostrophe.

Compound Words

A compound word is a word consisting of two or more words, for example a word processor (ordbehandlingsmaskin) (noun + noun)

Swedish usually writes compound nouns as one word; pendeltåg, affärsman, svärföräldrarna. English does not usually write compound nouns as one word, but there are no fixed rules.

1 As one word: businessman, boyfriend, knitwear
   These are always common and well-established compounds.
2 As two words: commuter train, steel production, chewing gum
   This is the usual way of writing English compound nouns.
3 With a hyphen: a well-known man, a tax-free grant
   A hyphen is always used with a compound adjective before a noun.
   British English sometimes uses a hyphen in compound nouns: parents-in-law.
   There seem to be no fixed rules.

The best advice we can give you is: write compound nouns as two words unless you are sure they are written as one word. Avoid hyphens except in compound adjectives before nouns. You can always check in a good dictionary.

Word Division

Another problem is how to divide words at the end of a line. The rules are different in Swedish and English, and the best advice is: Do not divide words. If you must divide a word, look it up in an English dictionary, for example *The Advanced Learner's Dictionary*, which shows you where words can be divided.

You will also find spelling rules in *Engelsk Universitetsgrammatik*: Skrivregler, pp. 432–39.

Composition Check List: Grammar, Punctuation and Spelling

Before you hand in a composition, whether in class or in an exam, you should take time to check certain language points. The most common mistakes, which you should look for in your compositions, are noted below, with the correct forms on the left and mistakes on the right. We have graded the mistakes from −1 to −4 to give you some idea of which are the most elementary ones (−4).

Grammar

1 Check the verbs in each sentence.

  a Check that each verb agrees with its subject. Mistakes of this kind, though very elementary, are common. Use the following table as a reminder of Present tense Subject-Verb agreement:

He, she, it is/was/has/does/
       wants etc.

They are/were/have/do/want etc. (All mistakes −4)

Note:
Everybody/Everyone is/was etc.

Be particularly careful where the subject-verb agreement is confused by the words that follow the subject, for example:

1 Students at a university often *think*...	(thinks	−4)
2 One problem that faces all students *is*...	(are	−4)
3 Anyone with these problems *believes*...	(believe	−4)
4 One of the main disadvantages *is*...	(are	−4)

  b Check that you have the right verb form and tense.

1 If this *happens*, there will be a great improvement.	(will happen	−4)
2 It describes how we *should* behave.	(shall	−4)
3 The balloon *rose*.	(raised	−4)
4 They succeeded *in doing* so.	(to do	−4)
5 They do not *want us to try*.	(want that we	−4)
6 It *consists* of...	(is consisting	−4)
7 In America they *are now* experimenting...	(now experiment	−4)
8 If this *were* true...	(would be true	−4)

c Check that each verb is written in formal style. Not *don't* but *do not*, not *can't* but *cannot* – unless you are deliberately writing colloquial English.

2 Check that all pronouns clearly refer back to the right noun in the previous phrase or sentence. Make sure that pronouns are used consistently. Look particularly carefully at sequences of references like people – they; we – our; you – your; one – one's. And make sure that *This* is used without ambiguity. It may need a noun to make the reference clear.

3 Check other grammatical points that are common causes of mistakes. Here are a few examples:

Articles
Society is wrong.	(the society	−2)
They were done in *the wrong way*.	(a wrong way	−2)
Housewives in Britain.	(the housewives	−2)

Countable and uncountable nouns
The *information* did not help.	(informations	−4)
He found it difficult to get *a job*.	(a work	−4)

Pronouns
A great many people	(a great deal of	−2)
There is a great difference.	(it is	−4)
Houses *which* were built	(who	−4)

Adjective/Adverb
It was *unusually* well planned	(unusual	−4)
They played *well*.	(good	−4)

Word order
Unfortunately *he was* wrong.	(was he	−4)
Not until then *did she realise* . . .	(she realised	−4)

Prepositions
The war went on *for* years.	(during	−2)
They met *at* a hotel.	(on	−4)
She was not interested *in* him.	(of	−2)

Punctuation

4 Check that you have used appropriate punctuation. Do not write run-on or incomplete sentences. Check the commas in particular. See Punctuation, p. 94–99.

Spelling

5 Check every word whose spelling you are uncertain about. Use a dictionary if you are at home or in class. Spelling mistakes in common words look particularly bad and get −2. See Spelling, p. 100–103.

Layout

6 Check that the layout is correct. Is there a title and is it underlined? Is there a margin on the left-hand side? Are the paragraphs clearly marked with indented first lines or double spacing?

All this checking will take some time, but it will be time well spent, both in your term compositions and in the exam. Gradually you will find that you are making fewer mistakes because you will have learnt through making your own corrections.

Key to Exercises

Exercise 5

1 The Old Town.
2 The long holidays teachers get.
3 A list of reasons for having commercial TV in Sweden.
4 A list of reasons for *not* having commercial TV in Sweden.
5 A list of the advantages of big city life.
6 A list of the advantages of living in the country.
7 A definition and exemplification of wish fulfilment.
8 The ways in which air pollution has a bad effect on the environment.
9 A list of arguments against day nurseries – probably followed by a list of arguments *for*
10 A brief retell of the story of the book, showing how simple it is.

Exercise 7

Summaries: "You describe your grandfather, who you thought was very strange and mysterious."
"Your grandfather impressed you very much because he was a character who looked big and did shocking things."

Comments: "I liked all the horrible details. They brought him to life."
"The story about the rabbit makes a good ending – it's a kind of climax to all the other shocking things he does."

Questions: "What did you mean by 'going to see a man about a dog'? Can't you explain a bit more why he was a mystery to you? What else did he do?"
"You seem to change your attitude to him in the middle – from 'a complete mystery' to 'a character'. Perhaps you could concentrate more on the idea of 'a character' as the main theme, but keep the mystery bit too. By the way, how old were you at this time?"

Exercise 8

1   This sentence has been added to bring the welfare officer to life and to explain the student's surprise.
2   This sentence now starts a new paragraph dealing with the development of the relationship.
3   This sentence has been moved up, to become the topic sentence for the ideas in the second paragraph.
4–5 These sentences have been added to explain why the development was slow.
6   This sentence has been changed to link it more logically to the topic sentence.
7   This new sentence explains the previous one.
8   This sentence has been rephrased to fit the main idea of the paragraph announced in the topic sentence.
9   A third paragraph marks the change from past to present time. The sentence has been polished a little.
10 The beginning of the sentence is changed to make it more logical.
11 The last sentence now gives a more logical explanation of the conclusion: I was able to learn that I am not the only pebble on the beach.

Exercise 11

1 *The major political parties in Sweden* is the topic of this paragraph. Therefore sentences 3, 5, 7 and 9 are irrelevant and should go.
2 *American tourists in Stockholm* is announced as the topic of this paragraph by the topic sentence. Therefore sentences 3 and 4 should be deleted.

Exercise 12

1 The first sentence, the question, is the topic sentence. Sentence 2 supports the topic sentence by answering, explaining it. Sentences 3 and 4 support Sentence 2 by illustrating "harmless" and "cheap" respectively. Sentence 5 supports the topic sentence again by introducing a new reason. Sentences 6 and 7 support Sentence 5 by explaining and illustrating it.

2 The first sentence is the topic sentence. Sentence 2 develops the idea of "threatening" and is supported in turn by Sentences 3 and 4, which explain the reactions.

3 The second sentence is the topic sentence. The first sentence introduces the subject by quoting the opinion of a native Londoner on the subject of English theatre. Sentences 3 and 5 tell us who cares. Sentence 4 gives evidence for the fact that audiences care, and the last sentence states the result of people caring.

4 First paragraph: The first sentence is the topic sentence. Sentence 2 gives us a reason why the employed mother was criticised, and Sentence 3 tells us who criticised her. Second paragraph: The second sentence is the topic sentence, because it functions as a parallel of the topic sentence in paragraph 1, i.e. it states the opposite situation. Sentence 1 functions as a bridge or transition to the topic sentence. Sentences 3 and 4 tell us how housewives feel about the new attitudes toward them. Sentence 5 states the reason for these new attitudes.

Exercise 14

Here are some suggestions for linking the sentences. There are other possible alternatives as well.

1 Because people eat, drink and smoke too much, they are not very fit.
People eat, drink and smoke too much, so they are not very fit.

2 The Government is beginning to realize that something is wrong, but it does not know what to do about it.
Although the Government is beginning to realize that something is wrong, it does not know what to do about it.

3 Without wasting any time, the inspector left because he had seen all he wanted to see.
Having seen all he wanted to see, the inspector left without wasting any time.

4 Realizing his mistake, Washington changed his plan.
Since Washington realized his mistake, he changed his plan.
As soon as Washington realized his mistake, he changed his plan.

5 The Allied Forces invaded Europe on June 6, supported by an intense air and naval bombardment.
The Allied Forces, who were supported by an intense air and naval bombardment, invaded Europe on June 6.

6 The headmaster did not want to go ahead with the plan until he had heard his colleagues' opinion.
Since the headmaster wanted to hear his colleagues' opinion first, he did not go ahead with the plan.

7 Until/unless society changes its attitudes to addicts, there will be no chance of improving the drug situation.
Society will have to change its attitudes to addicts if there is to be a chance of improving the drug situation.

8 Although it had several advantages, the scheme was abandoned.
Despite several advantages, the scheme was abandoned.

9 The Government was sensitive to public opinion, so it commissioned a Gallup poll.
Being sensitive to public opinion, the Government commissioned a Gallup poll.

10 Because the author does not present his story in the usual chronological order, but switches from past to present, and back again, it is very confusing.

Exercise 15

Suggested paragraph (but there are many equally good solutions)

This is a new publicity scheme which, although not yet tried out, promises very well. The Government is giving it both its moral and its financial support, but its success will depend, of course, on its reception by the public, whose reactions are always difficult to predict. Similar ideas have been launched in the past with little success, but the supporters of this scheme say that it has avoided all the weaknesses of its predecessors. It is sure to be successful.

Alternative paragraph

This is a new publicity scheme which has not yet been tried out but which promises well, so the Government is giving it both its moral and its financial support. Its success will depend, of course, on its reception by the public, whose reactions are always difficult to predict. Although similar ideas have been launched in the past which have had little success, its supporters say that, because it has avoided all the weaknesses of its predecessors, this scheme is sure to be successful.

Exercise 16

Work expands so as to fill the time available for its completion. *For example*, an elderly lady of leisure can spend an entire day in writing and dispatching a postcard to her niece at Bognor Regis. *Thus* a lack of real activity does not result in leisure. *On the contrary*, the thing to be done swells in importance in a direct ratio with the time to be spent.

Exercise 17

The various linking words and phrases are italicised.
To begin with, the defence of the English language has nothing to do with archaism, *or* with the setting up of a 'standard English' *which* must never be departed from. *On the contrary*, it is especially concerned with the scrapping of every word or idiom *which* has outworn its usefulness. It has *nothing to do with* correct grammar and syntax, *which* are of no importance so long as one makes one's meaning clear, *or* with the avoidance of Americanisms, *or* with what is called 'having a good style'. *On the other hand*, it is not *concerned with* fake simplicity *and* the attempt to make written English colloquial. *Nor* does it even imply in every case preferring the Saxon word to the Latin one, *though* it does imply using the fewest and shortest words *that* will cover one's meaning. *What is above all needed* is to let the meaning choose the word, *and* not the other way about.

Exercise 18 A

Paragraphing: There is no *visible* division of the material into logical units. Nearly every sentence starts on a new line as if it were a separate paragraph.

Unity: There is no *real* division into logical units, either. Each sentence jumps from one problem of the working woman to the next without any evident connection. There is no unity. In fact, the passage reads more like notes in preparation for a composition than a final version.

Coherence: We can perhaps guess what the connections between the ideas might be, but as they are not stated by means of various linking devices, there is a lack of coherence.

Exercise 18 B

This version is easier to read because it is more coherent. First, the visible division of the text into three paragraphs signals to the reader that there are three main ideas. Second, each paragraph is introduced by a topic sentence which clearly establishes the new main idea. Third, the sentences within each paragraph all support the main idea. The paragraphs are unified. Fourth, logical link words and phrases at the beginning of the sentences and within them show the logical connections. The reader does not have to guess them. Look at the function of these words and phrases in the text: *As I shall attempt to show, In other words, This means that, Another reason, namely, therefore, also*.

Exercise 19

Are Families Necessary?

"The family, with its narrow privacy and its tawdry secrets, is the source of all our discontent". When Edmund Leach, the Cambridge anthropologist, said *this*, there was an outcry from the defenders of the *family*. *He* was felt to be striking at the very roots of civilised society. *In fact*, Dr Leach wanted to shake us into some fresh thinking about the structure of the family in the age of working wives, the Pill and the social equality of men and women.

this refers back to the opening quotation, which has clearly established the subject of the article.
family links clearly, by repetition, with the opening quotation
The *sentence order* gives the implicit meaning "because he . . ."
He refers back to Edmund Leach.
In fact introduces a contrasting explanation of Dr Leach's statement.

Even the most tenacious champions of traditional family values would admit that the intensity of family life can cause emotional disturbance from time to time. *But against this* they could point out the assistance and comfort that a family can provide when one is sick or in trouble. *Unfortunately* families today tend to be

Even links and compares the attitudes of the defenders of family life and its critics. *Even* here contains the idea of *surprisingly enough*.
But against this introduces a contrasting argument.

Unfortunately states the writer's attitude to the fact he states.

small and widely scattered, *so that* the mutual assistance they can offer is limited. There is, *however*, an alternative to the nuclear family of children and parents living by themselves, *and this* is the extended family, represented in Britain today by the commune movement.

So that links cause and effect.

However introduces a solution which contrasts with the unfortunate fact stated in the preceding sentence.
and this is the link between an alternative and its definition.

Of course, the idea of replacing the nuclear family unit by *a larger group* is not a new *one*. There have been religious communities in the United States since the last century and in this century we have Russian and Chinese collective farms and the Israeli kibbutzim. *The latter* communities differ from those in Britain in one essential respect. *They* are all part of the structure of society in their particular country, *whereas* in Britain the commune movement is very much anti- Establishment. Almost all communes *here* are, to a greater or lesser extent, aimed at changing the family-based structure of our society, *which* they feel is harmful to the human personality. *Certainly*, no one can deny that there are an increasing number of people who are finding the pressures of *contemporary society* too much for *them*. Problems *like* mental illness, drug addiction and alcoholism have their roots in the loneliness of *unhappy people* who cannot communicate and who feel that there is no one who cares.

Of course express the writer's assumption that the information is well-known to the reader.
a larger group refers back to the commune movement at the end of the previous paragraph.
one refers back to *the idea*.
The latter refers to the last three communities mentioned: the Russian, Chinese, and Israeli.
They refers to *the latter communities*.
whereas marks the contrast between the two types of community.

here refers back to *in Britain*.

which refers to *structure*, not *our society*.
Certainly expresses the author's firm belief in the following statement.

contemporary society echoes *our society* in the previous sentence.
them refers to *an increasing number of people*
like introduces the examples.
unhappy people echoes *people* in the previous sentece.

The commune movement blames family life for most of *these problems*.

These problems refers to the problems in the preceding paragraph.

They complain that the nuclear family unit is too enclosed, too isolated to be able to promote *caring* relationships between people. *They* claim that families just do not communicate properly with each other and that *this* leads to even more loneliness and isolation. *They* suggest that a better solution is a group of about a dozen adults, with or without children, who all live together. *As* a member of one commune in a London suburb said: "We aren't drop-outs. We believe that communes can make a real contribution to society".

They means (the members of) the commune movement. *They* is repeated in the following sentences to provide an echo link.

caring refers back to *cares* at the end of the previous paragraph.

This refers to the fact that families do not communicate with each other.

As introduces a quotation which describes what a commune is. Note, incidentally, how the writer uses quotations to open and close his argument.

Exercise 20

3   Three passions, simple but overwhelmingly strong, have governed my life: the longing for love, the search for knowledge, and unbearable pity for the suffering of mankind. These passions, like great winds, have blown me hither and thither, in a wayward course, over a deep ocean of anguish, reaching to the very verge of despair.

5   I have sought love, first, because it brings ecstacy - ecstacy so great that I would often have sacrificed all the rest of life for a few hours of this joy. I have sought it, next, because it relieves loneliness – that terrible loneliness in which one shivering consciousness looks over the rim of the world into the cold unfathomable lifeless abyss. I have sought it, finally, because in the union of love I have seen, in a mystic miniature, the prefiguring vision of the heaven that saints and poets have imagined. This is what I sought, and though it might seem too good for human life, this is what – at last – I have found.

2   With equal passion I have sought knowledge. I have wished to understand the hearts of men. I have wished to know why the stars shine. And I have tried to apprehend the Pythagorean power by which number holds sway above the flux. A little of this, but not much, I have achieved.

4   Love and knowledge, so far as they were possible, led upward toward the heavens. But always pity brought me back to earth. Echoes of cries of pain reverberate in my heart. Children in famine, victims tortured by oppressors, helpless old people a hated burden to their sons, and the whole world of loneliness, poverty and pain make a mockery of what human life should be. I long to alleviate the evil, but I cannot, and I too suffer.

1   This has been my life. I have found it worth living, and would gladly live it again if the chance were offered me.

Diagram illustrating the paragraph structure of the text from Bertrand Russell's *Autobiography*.

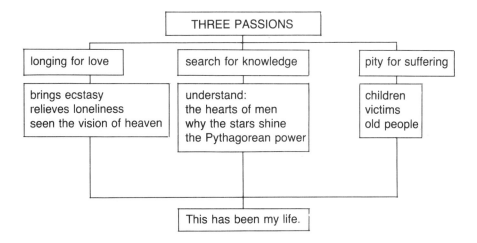

From this diagram you should be able to see how carefully, almost mathematically, Bertrand Russell has constructed his argument and with a large number of linguistic devices has linked his ideas together into a coherent and effective whole.

Exercise 21

The numbers at the end of each sentence refer to the rules on pp. 75–78.

1 Canterbury, which dates back to Roman times, has recently become a university town. (3)

2 One of the English towns which have Roman connections is Canterbury. (2)

3 Rosemary, who was still at school, was not expected home until later. (3)

4 He had two children who were still at school and one who was at university. (2)

5 It was none other than Benjamin Franklin that decided Thomas Paine's future for him. (1b)

6 *The Way of All Flesh*, which was not published until after Samuel Butler's death, is an autobiographical novel. (3)

7 He agreed to my suggestion, which surprised me very much. (4)

8 The library did not have the book which I wanted and which they had promised to get for me. (2)

9 The Minister assured them that there was no risk involved. (1a)

10 The committee wishes to point out that it does not approve of the scheme. (1a)

11 There is no doubt that the figures are correct. (1a)

12 They could not give one good reason why they should stay. (2)

13 The last suggestion is, in fact, the most feasible. (6)

14 Charlie Chaplin, the famous comedian, wrote his autobiography late in life. (5)

15 Darwin's contemporaries, however, were shocked by his theories. (6)

16 Sweden, like Britain, sought entry to the Common Market. (5)

17 At first sight, no doubt, these statistics look impressive. (6)

18 If, as we suspect, the decision was based on false premises, we must do our best to reverse it. (7)

19 A great deal of damage was done by the fire before it could be brought under control. (7)

20 Unfortunately, most of the building was damaged by water. (6)

21 However, the chapel was saved. (6)

22 When they left, the children remembered to thank their host. (7)

23 That was the position when William the Conqueror landed at Pevensey Bay. (7)

24 Since he ran the risk of being charged with treason, Buckingham fled to France. (7)

25 Lady Jane refused all offers to go into films although her sister, Lady Bird, is an actress at present appearing in a play in the West End. (5)

26 The candidate did not give a good impression. He looked as though he needed a shave; or: . . . impression; he looked . . . (9)

27 It was difficult to persuade them to leave. They insisted on staying to the bitter end; or: . . . . . . leave; they insisted . . . (9)

28 This is my advice: Don't. (11)

29 Sweden won several medals: one gold, two silvers and five bronzes. (11)

30 The fact that Amerigo Vespucci, a comparatively unknown Florentine, was the man who gave his name to the only continent that has been called after a person, has, however, often been quoted as an example of historical injustice. (1, 2, 5, 6)

Appendix I: Sample Compositions

A Student Composition
The Agony of Composition Writing

To produce a written piece of work is a rather complicated and frustrating task for a student who is not familiar with creating thoughts and ideas on paper. To be able to write spontaneously is not a natural development like learning to speak. It is a skill which requires motivation, imagination and concentration. Unfortunately, it is often taken for granted that students who are fluent in the spoken language should also be gifted with fluency in writing. However, this is not the case; to speak and to write are two totally different skills; a natural speaker is by no means a natural writer.

Confrontation with an exam in composition writing is a torment for the student who lacks the skill of writing. He cannot find a stimulating and appealing topic among the given subjects, neither can he create a satisfactory introduction to his written work. In order to succeed in a well-written composition, the student has to acquire confidence in his ability to write. He has to develop an interest in expressing himself on paper, and he has to find a purpose for his activity. Unsatisfactory and uninteresting subjects could easily destroy the inspiration to write, and without inspiration, no composition will be successful. Topics must be given to encourage the student to write something that he feels for and that is worth writing about. A free choice, for example, offers the student an opportunity to develop and express ideas that are important and significant to the writer himself. Guidance could be provided to the student who has difficulties in writing. This could be done in the form of given facts, to base the student writing on. It would help the unimaginative writer as well as the student who lacks ideas of his own. An introductory paragraph is another form of guidance that could be given to help the student who finds it hard to begin a composition.

It should be remembered that all students have not had the same opportunity to develop an acceptable skill in writing, as the importance given to composition writing varies among different teachers. It is the teacher's duty to find out the students' backgrounds in writing practice, in order to guide and assist their immediate needs. All students cannot achieve a high standard of imaginative writing, but the aim should be that the student is able to write what he wants to say with precision and clarity. (400 words)

Ingela Löfström

A CV (Curriculum Vitae)

A rather special kind of composition is a CV, or curriculum vitae. *Curriculum vitae* is the Latin for "course of life" and it is the brief description of yourself which you usually have to send in when you apply for a job or a scholarship in England or the U.S.

The function of a CV is, on the one hand, to let your future employer or sponsor see what sort of a person you are and how well you can express yourself in writing; and, on the other hand, to let you present yourself in your own words as the right person for the job or the scholarship.

Read the following CV, which is part of an application for a scholarship to study at an American university, and then discuss it with the help of the questions.

Curriculum vitae: Monica Sinclair

I was born on January 15, 1966 at Brighton on the south coast of England, where I spent the first five years of my life. I then moved with my family to Wembley, a suburb of London. My family consists of my father, a bank clerk, my mother, who stays at home and looks after us, an elder brother, who is studying to be a solicitor and a younger sister, who is still at school.

After primary school I went to the local comprehensive school in Wembley at the age of eleven. I did well both in school work and in the outside school activities, playing tennis and swimming in the school team. At the age of 19 I passed the GCE A levels in three subjects and now hope to go to university to get a degree in English. For the last six months I have been working as a receptionist at a hotel, and I was also an au pair girl in France for three months.

My main interests are literature, sport and travelling. Apart from my three months in France, I visited Germany in the summer of 1984 and last summer I attended a course on European literature in Paris. I really enjoy visiting foreign countries, because the experience of living in a different cultural environment makes you think twice about your own way of life.

I am looking forward to going to university next autumn, after which I hope to become a teacher. The reason why I am applying for a scholarship to go to an American college is that I know far too little about American literature, and it is difficult to understand the literature of a country unless one has lived there and come to understand its values and way of life.

Points to discuss

1 How has Monica organised her CV? Give "titles" for each of her four paragraphs.
2 If you were on the scholarship selection committee, would you feel she was worth a scholarship? Do you think she presents herself in the best possible light? What do you think she might have added?

A Composition Plan

For and Against Using Animals to Test New Medicines

1 Introduction of subject and problem:

In recent years a lot of people have been feeling unhappy about the suffering caused to animals by medical experiments; e.g. demonstrations in England.

2 Arguments against:

There are a number of good arguments behind these protests:
animals are dependent on us
animals feel pain
drugs have unpleasant side effects
some tests are not for real drugs but for cosmetics

3 Arguments for:

On the other hand, there are good reason for these experiments:
animals do not have minds like human beings
we might have to use human subjects for tests otherwise

4 Conclusion and personal opinion:

Efforts to stop tests are based on misplaced sentimentality. It is essential that we go on using animals in medical research.

Note that you normally put the arguments that you believe in last (here Arguments for). In this way you use them to knock down the arguments that you think are less convincing (here Arguments against). In the conclusion you state your own conclusion based on these arguments.

Exercise

Now write similar plans for the following subjects:

1 Commercial Television in Sweden
2 Life in a Big City
3 English as a World Language

The Use of Animals for Medical Research

In recent years quite a number of people have been feeling unhappy about the suffering caused to animals by scientists who use them to test new drugs and medicines as well as new methods of treatment. One often reads letters to the newspapers protesting about such experiments, and there are even demonstrations against using animals for tests.

Of course, there are a number of well-meaning arguments behind these protests. As the animal lovers say, animals are dependent on us, and what is more, they can feel pain just as we do. And although we use animals to test medicines, many drugs, for example, thalidomide, still turn out to have dangerous side effects, because after all human beings and animals are not exactly the same as one another. Moreover, the animal lovers point out, some of the experiments are not for drugs at all, but for cosmetics like shampoos and skin lotions, which have no medical justification.

On the other hand, animals do not have minds like human beings. They do not remember past pain or foresee what will happen to them in the future in the same way as we do. Moreover, the great majority of experiments are carried out under conditions that do not cause great suffering. It must also be remembered that if we did not use animals, we might have to test drugs on convicts or helpless mental patients, as has happened in the U.S.

To sum up, it seems to me that efforts to stop tests on animals are based on misplaced sentimentality. If tests of this kind had never been carried out, we would not have developed the antibiotics and pain killers that have prevented so much human suffering. Thus it is essential that we should go on using animals in medical research. (300 words)

Catherine Sandbach-Dahlström

On Ralph's Leadership Qualities in *Lord of the Flies*

In William Golding's *Lord of the Flies*, the stranded boys elect Ralph as their leader in spite of the fact that Jack, as head of the choir boys, is the more obvious candidate. After several attempts, however, Jack finally succeeds in seizing power from Ralph and becomes a savage dictator who involves his band in both torture and murder. How does this happen? Is it because Ralph is not a good enough leader?

From the beginning it is clear that Ralph needs Piggy's help in deciding what to do. At one point, when his responsibilities begin to weigh heavily on him, he reflects "I can't think. Not like Piggy" (ch. 5). As the boys behave more and more irrationally, Ralph even starts having blank spots when he forgets what he was going to say, and again, it is Piggy who helps him out (ch. 8).

However, this does not mean Ralph is a total failure as a leader. On the contrary he has courage, he can be decisive, and there are several occasions when Golding points out that he behaves with "genuine leadership" (ch. 1, see also ch. 4). Indeed, when Jack makes a final attempt to get the boys to vote for him rather than Ralph, he fails completely (ch. 8).

Still, Jack does triumph in the end. And it seems to me that this is because Ralph actually relies too much on thinking. He tries, for example, to deal with the boys' fear of the beast by discussing it rationally; he even tries to take a vote on whether there are ghosts or not (ch. 5). Jack, on the other hand, exploits the irrational forces in the boys. Where Ralph offers the boys the dull hard work of keeping a fire going for a reward which is all too unreal – the dim possibility of rescue – Jack offers them immediate rewards: meat and a chance to express their fears and aggressions in the excitement of the hunt.

It seems to me, then, that Ralph's personal limitations actually do not matter. In his portrayal of Ralph, Golding is telling us rather that in times of crisis any leader who appeals to reason alone is bound to fail. People do not want to think about unpleasant truths or face a threatening future. They want to drown their fears in excitement and be freed from responsibility and, like these 'civilized' British boys, they will end up following the leader that offers them these things. (about 400 words)

Note that in compositions about literature you should not just retell the story of a book, but rather explore an *opinion* you have about an aspect of the work you are writing about. This opinion may well be the result of a question you ask yourself about the book, as is the case in the essay above.

Appendix II: Composition subjects

General

1 Many students travel abroad to improve their command of foreign languages. Discuss the various ways in which it is possible to spend a few weeks or longer abroad for this purpose; for example, as an au-pair, by working, by going on a course or as a tourist. Which, in your opinion, is the most effective way, and why?
Title: *Foreign Travel and Language Learning*

2 The cost of living is very high today and it is difficult for many people to manage their budget, especially those living on a limited income, students and pensioners, for example. What suggestions can you make to help people in this situation?
Title: *Making Ends Meet*

3 How important is what you eat to your well-being? To your health and to the pleasures of life? Discuss the role that food plays in life.
Title: *You Are What You Eat*

4 There have been many school reforms in Sweden over the past 25 years, but still there is criticism of the way schools function. Analyze some of the problems in schools today and suggest the changes you would like to make.
Title: *The School I Would Like to Have*

5 Educational systems all over the world expect pupils to make choices when they are 16 or even younger. Fifty years ago most of the most important choices in a person's life had already been made by the age of fifteen – if the individual had any choice at all. When do you think the individual can and should make important choices? Illustrate your answer with references to your own experience.
Title: *Choosing a Future*

6 What are the main functions of a university education today? How can they best be fulfilled in your opinion? You might like to discuss its function with

regard to research, vocational training, self-realization, citizenship and the development of standards of values.
Title: *The Functions of a University*

7 Television and radio have to a great extent taken over the function of the daily newspaper as a source of news. In spite of this fact, however, people still read newspapers. Why is this, do you think? What do you expect of your daily newspaper? Discuss the different sections of the paper – the editorial, foreign news, home news, sports, arts, advertisements and so on.
Title: *My Daily Newspaper*

8 Swedish Radio buys a great many television programmes from British and American television companies. Some of them succeed in presenting aspects of British and American life quite successfully, others offer a very distorted picture.
Take one or two such programmes and assess the accuracy of their portrayal of the environment they deal with and suggest in what way they are of interest to Swedish viewers.
Title: *Television Broadens the Mind*

9 "Commercial TV is the only hope left to Swedish television". Argue for and against this opinion. Consider the weaknesses and merits of the present monopolistic system and the programmes it produces. With reference to other countries' TV systems, consider what effects commercial TV might have in Sweden.
Title: *TV in Sweden*

10 "The cosmetic manufacturers are not selling cosmetics, they are selling hope ... We no longer buy oranges, we buy vitality. We do not buy just an auto, we buy prestige". (From Vance Packard, *The Hidden Persuaders*). Is this a fair comment on present-day consumers and advertisers? In your answer you might discuss the goals and methods of advertising today.
Title: *Advertisers and Consumers*

11 The Women's Liberation Movement works on four principles: equal pay, equal opportunity in jobs and education, free contraception and abortion, 24-hour nursery facilities. Some people find the movement too extreme, others think they do not go far enough. What is your opinion of the Women's Liberation Movement?
Title: *Women's Lib*

12 "Marriage is popular because it combines the maximum of temptation with the maximum of opportunity" (Shaw). "It is better to marry than to burn"

(St Paul). Marriage has been an institution since time immemorial, yet some people are suggesting that in the near future marriage, at any rate true, monogamous marriage, will either disappear or be unnecessary, and only very conservative people and societies will retain it. What are your views on the subject?
Title: *Marriage in Modern Society*

13 Compare any two districts in Britain or America with each other, or any district in Sweden with any district in Britain or America. Explain why you make your particular choice; make comparisons and contrasts between the scenery, the history, the industry, the culture and the people who live in each of these two districts.
Title: *Two Parts of the World*

14 There are many links between Sweden and both Britain and the United States: cultural, economic, linguistic, political, historical... Discuss any of these aspects of Anglo-Swedish or American-Swedish relations.
Title: *Britain and Sweden* or *America and Sweden*

15 "The history of the United States is the greatest success story that mankind has ever known". Would you agree or disagree with this statement? Discuss it with reference to one or more aspects of American development.
Title: *The Story of America*

16 English is increasingly becoming a world language. Why do you think this is so? What should be the characteristics of a world language?
Title: *English as a World Language*

17 What problems inside Sweden do you think are the most serious ones today? Describe several of them, try to explain their causes and suggest some possible solutions to them (for example, the housing shortage, unemployment, drug addiction, road accidents, hooliganism).
Title: *Problems in Present-day Sweden*

18 Write a report for a newspaper on: "Swedish Towns, Now and in the Future". If you wish, you can refer to the following problems: public transport; the density of traffic; the housing situation; the growth and expansion of cities; the individual's influence (or lack of it) on his environment; architecture.
Title: *Swedish Towns, Now and in the Future*

19 More and more refugees are making their way to Sweden in the hope of finding a better life here. This increasing stream of immigrants from countries with a different cultural background creates problems for both

the host country and the immigrants. Discuss some of these problems, suggest solutions and – if you like – comment on Sweden's immigrant policy.

Title: *Immigrants*

20 The gap between the rich and the poor nations of the world is widening every day. Can you suggest ways of closing this gap? What kind of aid would be bring about this end? Loans, technical aid, education, birth control, charity, for example?

Title: *Closing the Gap*

Literature

21 How important do you think the study of literature is to language learning? Should people learn a language before they study its literature, or is studying literature a vital part of learning a language? The arguments against learning about literature are that it is too difficult, the language of literature is not the language of everyday life and that many people find it boring. It is also claimed, however, that literature helps students to understand how people think in the foreign language and gives them insight into the cultural background of the language.

Title: *The Importance of Literature in Learning a Language*

22 Many writers start their career by writing about their own lives, often including their recollections of childhood and youth. Choose any such book you have read in English, and comment on the way in which the writer deals with childhood and youth.

Title: *Childhood and Youth in (the book you choose)*

23 If literature reflects society, one should learn something about a particular country by reading its literature. Give an account of one novel or play that you feel has taught you a good deal about Britain, America, or any other English-speaking country.

Title: *Literature as a Mirror of Society*

24 England has a long tradition of women writers, and in the last ten years more women writers than ever before have been acknowledged as leading novelists. Has this led to a new way of presenting life in literature, or do women novelists describe life in much the same way as men novelists do?

Title: *Life through the Eyes of Women Novelists*

25 Nearly all literature deals with some form of conflict: conflicts between people, conflicts within people, conflicts between people and Nature, conflicts between people with different ideologies. Choose one book that you have read recently and discuss the conflicts that are presented there and the ways in which they are resolved.

Title: *The Conflicts in (Title of the book you choose)*

26 "Personally I believe that most people are influenced far more than they would care to admit by novels, serial stories, films and so forth, and that from this point of view the worst books are often the most important, because they are usually the ones that are read earliest in life" (George Orwell, Boys' Weeklies).

Do you agree with this statement?

Title: *"Bad" Books*

27 Literature is an effective means of propaganda and a writer can be active in drawing attention to the problems his or her society faces. Discuss the role of any one writer and show how the social purpose of his or her writing is expressed in one or two books.

Title: *The Writer as the Conscience of His Time*

28 Certain novels are set in regions or countries where the setting – the natural scenery and physical surroundings – plays an important part in the book. Select and discuss one or two books in which you feel these factors are an important feature.

Title: The title of the book(s) you have chosen

29 In most modern novels there is usually one character with whom you find it easy to identify. Select one such character and describe her or him not merely as presented by the author but as you yourself experienced the character.

Title: *A Character with Whom I Can Identify*

30 Many novels and plays describe the relationship between two people: often a man and a woman. Describe and analyse any such relationship in a British or American novel or play. Trace the development of the relationship, and illustrate it with references to specific incidents in the book.

Title: *Two Characters*